THE DESSERT COOKBOOK

THE DESSERT COOKBOOK

MARLYN COHEN
MARIAN FOX BURROS,
Consultant

GALAHAD BOOKS · NEW YORK CITY

Library of Congress Catalog Card Number: 73-90625
ISBN 0-88365-115-7

Published by arrangement with Funk & Wagnalls

Formerly published as AFTER ALL, A Dessert Cookbook For Everyone

Printed in the United States of America

CONTENTS

INTRODUCTION

Of all the books produced since the remote ages by human talents and industry those only that treat of cookery are, from a moral point of view, above suspicion. The intention of every other piece of prose may be discussed and even mistrusted, but the purpose of a cookery book is one and unmistakable. Its object can conceivably be no other than to increase the happiness of mankind.

— JOSEPH CONRAD

COOKING HAS been my hobby for over twenty-five years and, since this is an age of specialization, I have concentrated on desserts. It occurred to me that cakes didn't just happen; they must have had a beginning in the past; and pies, ices, and puddings also must have evolved into their present form. Washington, D.C., is my home, so I had the enormous resources of the Library of Congress right on my doorstep and I started researching the history of desserts. Very little was documented on this subject and putting together the pieces gleaned from old history books, old cookbooks, and many other sources was like finding the solution to a giant puzzle. In this book I have tried to demonstrate the glorious past and fascinating present of the world of desserts.

To a devoted cook, baking is a never-ending source of satisfaction and accomplishment. To put many seemingly unrelated ingredients into a bowl and carefully blend them together, to put batter into pans, to set pans into the oven, is to have an exciting experience—producing a work of art—layers of luscious cake to be laced together with creamy frosting. Could Michelangelo create anything more impressive? Desserts are fashioned to please the eye as well as to satisfy the sweet tooth. A beautiful, tasty dessert can erase the effects of a mediocre main course. There isn't a hostess-cook who doesn't feel that it is her crowning glory.

I remember when, as a bride, I had my very first dinner guests. I labored long and lovingly over the menu and the *pièce de résistance* was a gorgeous chocolate pie. With a real sense of theater I gave the dessert a setting of my best silver, topped it with drifts of whipped cream and with great fanfare, carried this treasure in to the assemblage. Just as I approached the table I tripped on the rug and no Mack Sennett comedy ever produced a sorrier pie-throwing mess. Certainly I splattered the rug, my dress, and the guests—but most important was the flatness of the dinner without dessert. So I learned early in my married life that a meal without a happy ending is a sad tale indeed.

The imaginative hostess plans the proper ending to her carefully planned menu. A heavy, many-course dinner should have an ice or soufflé as its partner. A light supper should be accompanied by a succulent fruit pie or delicious layer cake. A morning gathering at home can pair a warm coffee cake with a cup of steaming coffee; an afternoon meeting can team tea with small cakes or cookies.

In the course of time the habits of people change. Today

everyone is diet conscious. I have found it most important to offer my family tasty, sweet desserts made either with sugar substitutes or with a caloric count that is minimal. Have you noticed that when dieters cheat on their calories they are almost certain to be downing a delicious dessert?

Through the years I have accumulated the recipes in this book with tender, loving care. Each one has not only been thoroughly tested but usually wolfishly devoured by friends and family alike.

I am indebted to those who have delved into family archives to give me their culinary treasures, and to the caterers who have let me in on their little secrets. I have spent years reading magazine cookery articles and cookbooks, collecting and sorting information, and grounding myself in "dessertery," but without the final help from Marian Burros—who, incidentally, dug into her own voluminous files—this book never would have seen the light of day, or many of the desserts the soft light of dinner table candles.

M. S. C.

Basic Baking Information

EQUIPMENT

Cake pans—Should be of good quality to insure evenly ris-
  ing cakes
2 8- or 9-inch round pans
1 8- or 9-inch square pan
4 oblong loaf pans—assorted sizes from 7 to 15 inches
1 10 × 15 × 1-inch jelly roll pan
1 13 × 9 × 2-inch sheet cake pan
1 large-muffin tin
1 small-muffin tin
1 8- or 9-inch pie pan
1 10-inch pie pan

1

1 9-inch tube pan—a doughnut shaped pan with funnel-type center
1 9-inch spring form—a mold that has removable sides
2 cookie sheets
3 mixing bowls of various sizes
Electric mixer (second set of beaters, if possible)
Set of Measuring cups
Set of Measuring spoons
Rotary beater or whisk
Rolling pin
Wooden mixing spoon
Slotted spoon
Rubber spatula
Wire racks for cooling purposes
1 cake tester

General Tips for Successful Cake Baking

1. Most ingredients should be held at room temperature for at least 30 minutes before using. Never use cold eggs; remove from refrigerator one hour before baking.
2. General Cake-Baking Procedures
   a. Cream butter or shortening until light and smooth.
   b. Add sugar to shortening and cream.
   c. Add eggs one at a time to butter and sugar mixture. Blend.
   d. Sift flour before measuring. Sift dry ingredients (flour, baking powder, baking soda, spices, et cetera) together. Add to above mixture, but do not beat too much once leavening agent is added. Too much beating deters the leavening process and also makes for a

coarse-textured cake. Beat just enough to blend all ingredients.

e. Liquid should usually be added alternately with dry ingredients.

f. Egg whites that are stiffly beaten should be gently folded into the batter by hand, using a rubber spatula, and not beaten in.

3. Unless otherwise directed, prepare pans for baking by covering sides and bottom lightly with shortening. Sprinkle with flour and turn upside down to remove excess flour. Do not grease pans for angel food or sponge cakes. If pans are new, butter them empty and put in 350° oven for 15 minutes. Wash them and they're ready to use.

4. Use recommended pan size because too thick or too thin spreading of the batter will change character of the cake.

5. Unless otherwise directed, preheat oven before baking. Preheating is setting the oven at indicated temperature 10 to 15 minutes prior to baking. Cakes are generally baked in a moderate oven varying from 325° F. to 375° F. Remember that timing is always approximate. Test cake by inserting a toothpick, wire, or cake tester in center. If it comes out with no batter adhering, the cake is done. Another test for doneness: press cake gently; if it springs back without leaving imprint, it is done. Put single pan of cake in center of rack for even heat.

6. Let cake cool on rack before removing from pan. Unless otherwise directed, don't frost a warm cake.

7. For fruit cake, bake until cake tests done when a cake tester is inserted in center portion. Bake at 300° F.—no higher; sometimes 275° F.

8. Loaf pan 9″ × 5″ × 3″ will hold 5 cups of batter and take 2 hours to bake.

3-quart tube pan or mold will hold 2½ quarts and baking time is 2½ to 3 hours to bake.

Empty 6-ounce juice cans hold ½ cup and batter takes 50 minutes.

Small cup cake pans hold a rounded tablespoonful of batter and take 20 minutes to bake. Larger pans take ⅓ cup of batter and take 40 minutes to bake.

Where It All Began

CAKES IN THE PAST

THE WORD "cake" has its origin in the old Norse language. Their word *kaka*, meaning "something round or lumpy," might be applied today to the attempts of some new cooks. From the beginning, cake was considered the food of the gods. The Egyptians made cakes in the form of animals, birds, and even humans, shaping breasts, arms, or whatever seemed most appropriate for the god they were honoring with gifts. The Greeks made honey cakes for their gods. Epicures of ancient Rome and Athens ate mixtures of baked flour and honey soaked in wine. As the years went on, the pastry cooks of the northern countries added eggs, butter, and salt.

In Elizabethan England, delicacies such as almond paste, marchpane (a favorite sweetmeat), and gingerbread were prepared for the table by the noblewoman herself or under her supervision. Cakes were known to Shakespeare, for in *A Comedy of Errors* he wrote, "Your cake is warm within." There must also have been cake failures at that time, for in Shakespeare's *Taming of the Shrew*, Gremio laments, "Our cake's dough on both sides." In 1623, in London, *The Countrey Contentments, a* book by Gervase Markham, printed a "receipt" for Spice Cake. The choicest cake as well as the first made without bread dough was the Nun's Cake concocted in honor of the wedding of a nobleman's daughter. The following highly prized cake recipe first appeared in 1747 in Hannah Glasse's *The Art of Cookery Made Plain and Easy:*

NUN'S CAKE (1747)

You must take four pounds of the finest flour, and three pounds of double refined sugar beaten and sifted; mix them together and dry them by the fire till you prepare your other materials. Take four pounds of butter; beat it with your hand till it is soft like cream, then beat 35 eggs, leave sixteen whites, strain off your eggs from the treads and beat them and the butter together till all appears like butter. Put in 4 or 5 spoonsful of rose or orange flowere water, and beat again, then take your flour and sugar with 6 ounces of carroway seeds and strew them in by degrees, beating it up all the time for two hours together. You may put in as much tincture of cinnamon or ambergrise as you please; butter your hoop and let it stand three hours in a moderate oven. You must observe always, in beating of butter, to do it with a cool hand and beat it always one way in a deep earthen dish.

NUN'S CAKE (1967)

1 cup butter, softened	½ tsp. salt
1½ cups powdered sugar	¾ cup milk
5 egg yolks	3 tsps. caraway seeds
2 egg whites	2 tsps. vanilla
3 cups flour	½ tsp. cinnamon
2½ tsps. baking powder	

Preheat oven to 350° F.

Butter well and flour a 9-inch cake pan.

Beat butter, sugar, and egg yolks until light and fluffy. Stir in unbeaten egg whites and beat one minute. Sift flour with baking powder and salt and add to egg mixture alternately with milk. Sprinkle in caraway seeds, beat well, and add flavoring. Pour into prepared cake pan. Bake 45 minutes.

Almost all cakes were first associated with specific events such as Twelfth Night or Mid-Lent. Quite a number were made and freely distributed according to the terms of a will or as a reminder of some unusual event, such as the cakes offered every Easter Monday in the village of Biddenden in Kent in memory of the Biddenden Maids, Siamese twins born in A.D. 1100. A device showing the maids was pressed onto the cakes.

A famous cookie, the Bosworth Humbel, is made from a recipe dropped by the chef of King Richard III at Bosworth Field, during the last battle of the War of the Roses, in which Richard was killed. Legend states that some resident found the recipe and these cookies have been made from it ever since.

The small Maid of Honour cakes date from 1525, when Henry VIII saw the Maids of Honour of Queen Catherine of Aragon relishing them. He tried one, found it delicious, and they became standard fare in his court.

Hampshire, Bath, and Shropshire vie as the "original home" of English gingerbread. There it was pressed into wooden molds, baked, and frosted. The early molds in Valentine shapes are still on display in the Bath Pump Room Museum.

Eventually the art of cakemaking came to France, where cake shops, established on Faubourg St. Honoré, became meeting places for gourmets. One such was owned by Julien Gouffé, whose family perfected the Trois-frères, Savarin, and Gorenflot, all of which are still made today.

Finally cake came to the shores of the New World. Early American cakes were sweetened with molasses from the West Indies, embellished with fruit from Spain and Italy, raisins and currants from the Mediterranean, and spices brought from all over the world by Dutch merchant-men. Eggs, of course, were produced in abundance and flour was made in the home, or ground at local grist mills.

America's big contribution to cake baking was the development of leavening agents. In the first American cookbook, *An American Lady*, published in 1805, the Cheap Seed Cake recipe used "emptins" as a leavening agent. Emptins were a substance made from hops or cornmeal leavings or sometimes dregs from cider. Occasionally the emptins were made from peach leaves, which fermented and produced a type of yeast that would make the cake rise. This word was in such common use that the Bigelow Papers stated: "Twill take more emptins by a long chalk to give such heavy cakes as these a start." Pearlash, commercial potassium carbonate, used in 1827, was also a form of emptins. Tartar and baking soda were introduced in the 1880's. Finally the use of baking powder was perfected and our elegant, delectable modern cake was made possible.

Cakes

CAKE PANS should be greased and floured before putting in the batter for baking, unless otherwise noted.

GREAT SCOTT DEVIL'S FOOD CAKE
Old Southern Recipe, My Favorite

¼ pound butter	2 cups flour, sifted
2 cups sugar	1 tsp. vanilla
2 eggs	2 tsps. baking soda
4 squares unsweetened chocolate	1 cup sour cream
	1 cup hot water

Preheat oven to 350° F.

Grease well and lightly flour three 9-inch layer-cake pans.

Cream butter and sugar; add eggs, one at a time, beating well after each addition. Melt chocolate; add chocolate,

9

flour, and vanilla to butter mixture. Add soda to sour cream, then fold into batter. Add hot water. Pour batter into prepared cake pans and bake for about 20 minutes. Cool in pans or on wire rack. Frost and fill with Fudge Frosting (page 29).

MOM'S FUDGE CAKE

3 squares unsweetened chocolate	2 eggs
½ cup milk	2 cups sifted flour
1 egg, well-beaten	1 tsp. baking soda
1⅔ cup sugar	1 tsp. salt
½ cup shortening	⅔ cup milk
1 tsp. vanilla	Walnuts for garnish

Preheat oven to 350° F.

Grease and flour two 9-inch layer-cake pans.

Combine chocolate, ½ cup milk, 1 well-beaten egg, and ⅔ cup sugar in saucepan. Cook over low heat until thickened, stirring constantly. Cool. Stir shortening to soften. Gradually add remaining sugar. Cream until light and fluffy. Add vanilla. Add remaining eggs one at a time, beating well after each addition. Add cooled chocolate mixture. Sift flour, soda, and salt together. Add flour mixture to creamed mixture alternately with ⅔ cup milk. Pour into prepared pans and bake for 25 to 30 minutes. Cool. Frost and fill with Chocolate Satin Frosting (p. 32) and garnish with walnut halves.

1-2-3-4 CAKE

1 cup butter	1 Tbs. baking powder
2 cups sugar	1 tsp. salt
4 eggs	1 cup milk
3 cups sifted flour	1 tsp. vanilla

Preheat oven to 350° F.

Grease and flour three 9-inch layer-cake pans.

Cream butter and sugar together until light and fluffy. Add eggs to the creamed mixture one at a time. Sift flour, baking powder, and salt together. Add flour mixture and milk alternately. Add vanilla. Pour into prepared pans and bake for 25 minutes. Cool. Frost and fill with Chocolate Butter-cream Frosting (p. 31).

MARBLE LAYER CAKE
Very light cake

3 cups sifted flour
1 Tb. baking powder
½ tsp. salt
¾ cup butter
2 cups sugar
¾ cup milk
1 tsp. vanilla

6 egg whites, stiffly beaten
3 squares (1-oz.) unsweetened chocolate, melted
4 Tbs. sugar
¼ cup boiling water
¼ tsp. baking soda

Preheat oven to 350° F.

Grease and flour two 9-inch layer-cake pans.

Sift flour, baking powder, and salt together. Cream butter thoroughly; add 2 cups sugar. Cream together until light and fluffy. Add sifted mixture alternately with milk, a small amount at a time, beating until smooth. Add vanilla. Fold in egg whites quickly and thoroughly. To melted chocolate add 4 tablespoons sugar, boiling water, and soda. Cool. Divide batter in half. Add cooled chocolate mixture to half of the batter. Spoon the light and dark batters alternately into prepared pans. Run a knife through the batter before baking. Bake for about 25 minutes. Cool. Fill and frost with Hungarian Chocolate Frosting (p. 29).

RING MARBLE CAKE
Texture of pound cake. Must use 9-inch ring mold

⅓ cup butter
1 tsp. vanilla
1 cup sugar
2 tsps. baking powder
2 cups sifted flour
¼ tsp. salt

⅔ cup milk
3 egg whites, stiffly beaten
1 square unsweetened
    chocolate
2 Tbs. hot water
¼ tsp. baking soda

Preheat oven to 350° F.

Grease and flour 9-inch ring mold.

Thoroughly cream butter, vanilla, and sugar. Add sifted dry ingredients alternately with milk. Fold in egg whites. Combine chocolate and water and melt. Add soda; blend. Divide batter in half. To one half add the chocolate mixture. Alternate light and dark batters by spoonfuls in prepared ring pan. Bake about 1 hour. Cool and frost with Chocolate Satin Frosting (p. 32).

MARTHA WASHINGTON DEVIL'S FOOD

4 squares unsweetened
    chocolate
1 cup sugar
½ cup buttermilk or sour
    milk
2½ cups sifted flour
1½ tsps. baking powder
¾ tsp. baking soda

½ tsp. salt
½ cup butter
¾ cup sugar
3 eggs
1 cup buttermilk or sour
    milk
1 tsp. vanilla

Preheat oven to 350° F.

Grease 9 × 15 × 2-inch baking pan.

Melt chocolate over boiling water; add 1 cup sugar and ½ cup buttermilk and stir over boiling water until sugar is dissolved. Cool. Sift flour, baking powder, soda, and salt together three times. Cream butter with ¾ cup sugar until light and fluffy. Add eggs and beat well. Add about ¼ of flour mixture; mix thoroughly; add chocolate and blend. Add remaining flour a little at a time alternately with remaining buttermilk; add vanilla. Pour into prepared pan and bake for 30 minutes. Cool. Frost with Fudge Frosting or Rich Chocolate Butter-cream Frosting (pp. 29, 31).

WELLESLEY FUDGE CAKE

4 squares unsweetened chocolate
½ cup hot water
½ cup sugar
2 cups sifted flour
1 tsp. baking soda
1 tsp. salt
½ cup butter or other shortening

1¼ cups sugar
3 eggs, unbeaten
1 tsp. vanilla
Milk (with butter or margarine use ⅔ cup. With any other shortening use ¾ cup)

Preheat oven to 350° F.

Grease and flour two 9-inch layer-cake pans or 8 × 12 × 2-inch sheet cake pan.

Place chocolate and water in top of double boiler. Cook and stir until chocolate melts and mixture thickens. Add ½ cup sugar and cook 2 minutes longer. Cool.

Sift flour, soda, and salt together 3 times. Cream shortening; add remaining sugar. Cream until light and fluffy. Add eggs one at a time, beating after each addition. Add chocolate mixture and blend. Add milk and vanilla alternately with sifted dry ingredients. Bake for 25 to 30 minutes; 40 minutes for loaf pan. Cool. Frost and fill with Fudge Frosting (p. 29).

JUBILEE LAYER CAKE

3 cups sifted flour	2 cups sugar
1 Tb. baking powder	3 eggs and 2 egg yolks
½ tsp. salt	1 cup milk
1 cup butter	1½ tsps. vanilla

Preheat oven to 375° F.

Grease and flour three 9-inch layer-cake pans.

Sift flour, baking powder, and salt together three times. Cream butter thoroughly. Add sugar gradually and cream together until light and fluffy. Add eggs and yolks and beat well. Add flour, alternately with milk, a small amount at a time, beating until smooth. Add vanilla. Pour into prepared pans and bake for 20 minutes. Cool. Frost and fill with Fluffy Seven Minute Frosting (p. 31).

DEVIL'S FOOD WALNUT CAKE

⅓ cup shortening	1 tsp. baking powder
1¼ cups brown sugar	½ tsp. salt
2 eggs, well beaten	¾ cup finely chopped
½ cup boiling water	walnuts
2 squares unsweetened	½ cup sour milk or
chocolate	buttermilk
1½ cups sifted flour	1 tsp. vanilla
1 tsp. baking soda	

Preheat oven to 350° F.

Grease and flour 8- or 9-inch ring pan or 9 × 5 × 3-inch loaf pan.

Cream shortening with sugar until light and fluffy. Add beaten eggs and beat well. Pour boiling water over chocolate and stir over low heat until smooth; cool. Add to egg mixture. Sift flour, soda, baking powder, and salt together. Add walnuts. Combine milk and vanilla and add to chocolate mixture alternately with the dry ingredients. Turn into prepared pan and bake for 50 to 60 minutes. Cool. Frost with Fluffy Seven Minute Frosting (p. 31).

DELICATE CHOCOLATE CAKE

1¾ cups sifted flour
1 tsp. baking soda
1 tsp. salt
1¼ cups sugar
½ cup shortening

2 eggs, separated
2 squares unsweetened chocolate
1 tsp. vanilla
1 cup buttermilk

Preheat oven to 350° F.

Grease and flour two 9-inch layer-cake pans.

Sift flour, soda, and salt together. Cream sugar and shortening together. Add egg yolks one at a time. Beat until fluffy. Melt chocolate and add creamed mixture; mix. Add vanilla to buttermilk. Add dry and liquid ingredients alternately to the creamed mixture. Mix thoroughly. Beat egg whites until stiff but not dry. Fold gently into batter. Turn into prepared pans and bake for about 30 minutes. Frost with Hungarian Chocolate Frosting (p. 29).

BANANA CAKE

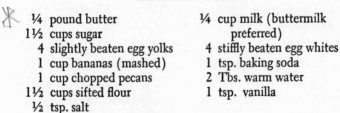

¼ pound butter
1½ cups sugar
4 slightly beaten egg yolks
1 cup bananas (mashed)
1 cup chopped pecans
1½ cups sifted flour
½ tsp. salt

¼ cup milk (buttermilk preferred)
4 stiffly beaten egg whites
1 tsp. baking soda
2 Tbs. warm water
1 tsp. vanilla

Preheat oven to 350° F.

Grease and flour two 9-inch layer-cake pans or a 10-inch tube pan.

Cream butter with sugar. Add egg yolks and beat. Add mashed bananas and pecans. Sift together flour and salt. Combine with creamed mixture, alternating with milk. Fold in beaten egg whites. Add soda dissolved in water and then vanilla. Bake for 25 to 30 minutes. Cool and frost with Pecan Cream Frosting (p. 31).

LAZY DAISY CAKE

2½ cups sifted flour
2½ tsps. baking powder
1 tsp. salt
1 cup milk
4 Tbs. butter

¼ tsp. grated lemon rind
2 tsps. lemon juice
4 eggs
1½ cups sugar

Preheat oven to 350° F.

Grease 10 × 10 × 2-inch pan.

Sift flour, baking powder, and salt together three times. Heat (do not scald) milk, butter, and lemon rind over low flame until butter is melted. Remove from heat and cool slightly. Add lemon juice to eggs and beat until thick and lemon-colored; add sugar gradually and beat until light and fluffy. Add flour, alternately with warm milk mixture, mixing quickly but thoroughly. Pour into pan and bake for 35 minutes. Immediately cover with Coconut Topping.

Coconut Topping

¾ cup light brown sugar
4 Tbs. cream

4 Tbs. melted butter
1 cup coconut

Combine sugar, cream, butter, and mix lightly until thoroughly blended. Stir in coconut. Spread evenly over top of cake. Return cake to oven for 12 to 15 minutes or until brown-sugar mix caramelizes. Keep eye on this so that it does not burn.

HONEY DEVIL'S FOOD CAKE

2 cups sifted flour
1 tsp. baking soda
¼ tsp. salt
½ cup butter or other
    shortening
½ cup sugar

¾ cup corn syrup
2 eggs or 3 egg yolks
2 to 3 squares unsweetened
    chocolate, melted
¾ cup milk
1 tsp. vanilla

Preheat oven to 350° F.

Grease two 9-inch layer-cake pans.

Sift flour, soda, and salt three times. Cream shortening with sugar. Add syrup and beat well. Add eggs one at a time, beating well after each; then add chocolate and blend. Add flour alternately with milk, beating after each addition until smooth. Add vanilla. Pour into prepared pans and bake for 25 minutes. Cool. Frost and fill with Fluffy Seven Minute Frosting (p. 31).

FRESH COCONUT CAKE

2¼ cups sifted flour
1½ cups sugar
4 tsps. baking powder
1 tsp. salt
½ cup butter
¾ cup coconut milk*

1 tsp. vanilla
4 egg whites, unbeaten
¼ cup coconut milk*
1 cup freshly grated coconut

Preheat oven to 350° F.

Into the bowl of an electric mixer sift the flour, sugar, baking powder, and salt. Add the butter, ¾ cup of coconut milk and vanilla. Beat for 2 minutes with mixer set at low to medium speed, scraping the bowl as required. Add egg whites and the remaining ¼ cup of coconut milk. Beat for 2 minutes. Turn batter into two 9-inch layer-cake pans, greased and lined with wax paper. Bake for 25 minutes. Cool cake before removing from pans. When cake is cool frost with either Fluffy Seven Minute Frosting (p. 31) or sweetened whipped cream. Sprinkle with freshly grated coconut.

---

* To extract milk, punch two holes in coconut with an ice pick and drain.

GOLDEN CREAM CHOCOLATE CAKE

2 cups sifted flour
2 tsps. baking powder
¼ tsp. soda
½ tsp. salt
½ cup butter or shortening
1¼ cups sugar

2 eggs, unbeaten
3 squares unsweetened
    chocolate, melted
1 cup milk
1 tsp. vanilla

Preheat oven to 350° F.

Grease and flour two 9-inch layer-cake pans.

Sift flour. Add baking powder, soda, and salt and sift again. Cream butter and add sugar. Cream until light and fluffy. Add eggs, one at a time, beating after each addition. Add melted chocolate. Add flour alternately with milk, beating until smooth. Add vanilla. Pour into prepared pans and bake for 30 minutes. Cool. Frost with Hungarian Chocolate Frosting (p. 29).

THREE EGG YOLK GOLD CAKE

2 cups sifted flour
1 Tb. baking powder
¼ tsp. salt
½ cup butter
1 cup sugar

3 egg yolks
¾ cup milk
½ tsp. grated orange rind
    (optional)

Preheat oven to 375° F.

Grease and flour two 8-inch layer-cake pans.

Sift together flour, baking powder, and salt three times. Cream butter with sugar until mixture is light and fluffy. Add egg yolks, which have been beaten until very thick and lemon-colored, to creamed mixture. Beat well. Add the flour mixture alternately with the milk, beating smooth after each addition. Stir in orange rind. Pour into prepared pans and bake for 25 to 30 minutes. Cool. Frost and fill with Hungarian Chocolate Frosting (p. 29).

PINEAPPLE CHIFFON CAKE

2¼ cups sifted flour
1½ cups sugar
1 tsp. salt
1 Tb. baking powder
½ cup salad oil

5 unbeaten egg yolks
¾ cup unsweetened pine-
    apple juice
1 cup egg whites
½ tsp. cream of tartar

Preheat oven to 325° F.

Sift dry ingredients into mixing bowl and make a well in middle. Add salad oil, egg yolks, and pineapple juice in given order. Beat until smooth. Combine egg white and cream of tartar in large bowl. Beat until they stand in stiff peaks when beater is lifted from bowl. Fold into egg-yolk batter. Pour into greased and floured 9- or 10-inch tube pan. Bake for 55 minutes, then increase heat to 350° F. for 10 minutes. Cool. Frost with Pineapple Cream Frosting (p. 30).

HAPPY BIRTHDAY COCONUT CAKE

2¼ cups sifted flour
2½ tsps. baking powder
1½ cups sugar
1 tsp. salt
¾ cup butter
½ cup milk

1 tsp. grated orange rind
½ tsp. almond extract
1 egg
¼ cup milk
2 eggs
Shredded coconut

Preheat oven to 375° F.

Grease and flour two 9-inch layer-cake pans.

Sift first 4 ingredients together into mixing bowl. Add softened butter, ½ cup milk, orange rind, almond extract, and 1 unbeaten egg. Beat well 2 minutes by hand or in mixer at low speed. Add ¼ cup milk and 2 unbeaten eggs. Pour into prepared pans. Bake 25 to 30 minutes. Cool. Frost with Fluffy Seven Minute Frosting (p. 31). Top with coconut.

FRUITED MOCHA LAYER CAKE

2 cups sifted flour
3 Tbs. cocoa
2¼ tsps. baking powder
¼ tsp. salt
½ cup butter
1 cup sugar
1 egg, well beaten
¾ cup strong coffee

1 tsp. vanilla
2 Tbs. confectioner's sugar
1 cup heavy cream, whipped
½ cup seedless raisins
½ cup broken nuts
Confectioner's sugar for topping

Preheat oven to 375° F.

Grease two 9-inch layer-cake pans.

Sift flour with cocoa, baking powder, and salt. Cream butter and add sugar gradually, creaming until light and fluffy; then beat in egg. Add flour mixture alternately with coffee, a small amount at a time, beating until smooth. Add vanilla. Pour into prepared pans and bake for 30 minutes. Cool.

Filling

Fold confectioner's sugar into whipped cream until blended. Fold in raisins and nuts. Spread between layers of cake. Sprinkle confectioner's sugar lightly over top of cake.

BABETTE'S PUMPKIN CAKE

⅔ cup sugar
⅔ cup butter
4 eggs, beaten
1 pound canned pumpkin
⅔ cup water
3⅓ cups sifted flour
½ tsp. baking powder

2 tsps. baking soda
1½ tsps. salt
½ tsp. cloves
1 tsp. cinnamon
⅔ cup chopped walnuts
⅔ cup cut-up dates

Preheat oven to 350° F.

Grease and flour 9 × 5 × 3-inch loaf pan.

Cream together sugar and butter until light and fluffy. Add eggs, pumpkin, and water. Sift together flour, baking powder, soda, salt, and spices. Gradually stir dry ingredients into pumpkin mixture. Add nuts and dates. Blend well. Pour into prepared pan and bake for 1 hour and 15 minutes.

STRAWBERRY ALASKA CAKE

1¼ cups sifted flour
¾ cup sugar
2½ tsps. baking powder
½ tsp. salt
⅓ cup butter
4 egg yolks, unbeaten
½ cup milk

1½ tsps. vanilla
¼ cup milk
1 cup heavy cream, whipped
1 pint strawberries, sliced
    and sweetened
Whole berries

Preheat oven to 350° F.

Grease and flour two 8-inch square layer pans.

Sift flour, sugar, baking powder, and salt into mixing bowl. Cream butter and egg yolks until light. Add ½ cup milk and 1½ teaspoons vanilla. Blend. Fold in flour mixture and mix 2 minutes in electric mixer at low speed. Scrape bowl. Add ¼ cup of milk. Beat again. Put batter in prepared pans. Cover with meringue.

Meringue

4 egg whites
⅛ tsp. cream of tartar

1 cup sugar
¼ tsp. vanilla

Beat egg whites until frothy, add cream of tartar, then beat until stiff. Beat in sugar gradually, a tablespoon at a time. The final mixture should be very thick and stiff. Add vanilla. Spread evenly over batter in pans. Bake for 40 to 45 minutes or until meringue is firm and delicately brown. Cool and remove from pans.

Spread half of whipped cream on meringue side of 1 layer and cover with berries. Put other layer on top and cover with rest of cream. Garnish with whole berries.

SERVES 6 to 8

SEASON'S GREETINGS DARK FRUITCAKE
Very little cake, but loaded with fruit

½ lb. butter	1 lb. figs, cut up
1 lb. brown sugar	1 lb. dates, cut up
1 cup flour	1 lb. cooked prunes, cut up
2 tsps. baking powder	1 lb. currants
1 tsp. nutmeg	1 lb. mixed chopped candied
2 tsps. cinnamon	fruit
½ tsp. cloves	½ lb. candied halved cherries
½ tsp. allspice	½ lb. pecans, chopped a little
6 extra-large eggs, separated	¼ lb. blanched halved
½ cup wine or fruit juice*	almonds
3 cups flour (about)	1 cup walnuts
1 lb. golden raisins	Juice, rum, or brandy
1 lb. seedless raisins	(optional)

Preheat oven to 350° F.

Grease and line with waxed paper two 4 × 8½-inch loaf pans.

Cream butter and sugar. Add 1 cup flour, sifted with baking powder and spices. Add beaten yolks, then fold in the stiffly beaten egg whites. Add wine or juice. Using 3 cups of flour [more or less as needed], mix small quantities of fruit and nuts with it and add gradually to batter.

If more cake than fruit is preferred, then omit the currants and figs. Turn cakes into prepared pans and bake for 10 minutes. Then reduce heat to 300° F. and bake for 1 to 2 hours, depending on the size of the cake. Cool and sprinkle liberally with juice, rum, or brandy. Then wrap in foil and store.

DOBOSCH TORTE

7 eggs, separated	1 cup sifted cake flour
¾ cup sugar	¼ tsp. salt
1 tsp. vanilla	

---

* Any wine that is not excessively sweet.

Preheat oven to 350° F.

Butter the bottom of three 8- or 9-inch spring-form pans or two 8- or 9-inch layer-cake pans. Cover with rounds of wax paper and butter the paper.

Beat egg yolks with sugar until light and pale in color. Add vanilla. Fold in flour with salt. Beat egg whites until stiff but not dry and fold them gently through batter. Put 5 or 6 tablespoons of the batter into each pan and spread evenly. Bake for about 8 minutes. Cool and remove wax paper. Repeat until all the batter is used and 8 or 10 layers have been baked and cooled. Put layers together with chocolate cream and frost with same. Chill thoroughly. Then pour on glaze.

Chocolate Cream

6 eggs	4 Tbs. water
1 cup sugar	1 cup soft butter
5 squares unsweetened chocolate	

Beat eggs until fluffy, add sugar, and beat the mixture over hot water until it thickens. Remove from the heat and stir in unsweetened chocolate which has been melted with 4 tablespoons of water. Beat in, bit by bit, 1 cup soft butter. Chill the cream before using.

Glaze

½ cup sugar	½ cup water
1 tsp. lemon juice	⅝ cup sugar

Melt ½ cup sugar with 1 teaspoon lemon juice and cook slowly until golden brown. Stir in water and ⅝ cup sugar. Bring to a boil and cook to the soft-crack stage (270–285° F.) determined by dropping a little mixture into cold water. Pour this glaze over chilled cake, spread quickly with hot spatula, and mark into sections with knife dipped in hot water.

PEACH CAKE

1 cup flour, sifted
1 tsp. baking powder
¾ tsp. salt
2 eggs
1 cup sugar
½ cup milk

1 Tb. butter
About 4 peaches
Confectioner's sugar,
   enough to cover lightly
Apricot jam

Preheat oven to 350° F.

Grease and flour 9-inch spring form.

Sift together flour, baking powder, and salt. Beat eggs for at least 10 minutes until they are the consistency of mayonnaise. Gradually add sugar to eggs and then stir in sifted dry ingredients. Heat milk and butter until warm and add to batter. Pour into prepared spring form and bake for 35 minutes. Carefully remove cake from oven and arrange unpeeled peach sections, skin side down, on the top of the cake. Sprinkle fruit with sugar. Bake 10 to 15 minutes longer. Cool in the pan. Brush fruit with apricot jam and sprinkle heavily with sifted confectioner's sugar just before serving.

MARTHA WASHINGTON'S GREAT CAKE
Makes 11 pounds

1 lb. golden raisins
1 box (11-oz.) currants
1 cup candied orange peel
¾ cup candied lemon peel
1 cup citron
⅓ cup candied angelica
⅓ cup candied red cherries
⅓ cup candied green cherries
½ cup brandy

4½ cups sifted flour
1 tsp. mace
½ tsp. nutmeg
1 lb. softened butter
2 cups sugar
10 eggs, separated
2 tsps. fresh lemon juice
⅓ cup sherry

A day ahead: Pick over raisins and currants; soak overnight in water. Chop orange, lemon peel, citron, angelica, red and green cherries quite fine. Pour brandy over fruit and allow to stand overnight.

Preheat oven to 350° F.

Grease and flour 10-inch tube pan, 10-inch Turk's head mold, or two 9 × 5-inch loaf pans.

The following day sift together flour, mace, nutmeg. Set aside. Work butter until creamy, then add one cup sugar, a little at a time, beating until smooth. Beat egg yolks until thick and light, then beat in remaining cup of sugar, a little at a time, and the lemon juice. Combine with butter-sugar mixture. Add flour and sherry alternately. Stir in all the fruit and, last of all, fold in stiffly beaten egg whites.

Pour batter into prepared pan. Place pan of hot water in bottom of oven. Place cake pan(s) on racks in oven and bake for 20 minutes. Reduce heat to 325° F. and continue baking for 1 hour and 40 minutes for large cake; 40 minutes for loaf cakes. Cakes are done when a cake tester or toothpick inserted in center comes out dry. Turn out onto a rack and cool. Wrap in cheesecloth soaked in sherry or brandy and store in an airtight container for a month or more. When cheesecloth dries out, soak again with the same spirits and rewrap cake.

HAWAIIAN PUKA CAKE
Puka means holes

1 box Lemon Velvet Cake Mix
1 small package lemon gelatine
4 medium eggs
¾ cup liquid shortening
¾ cup pineapple juice
2 cups confectioner's sugar
4 Tbs. pineapple juice

Preheat oven to 350° F.

Mix first five ingredients well. Pour into greased and floured 9 × 13 × 2-inch pan. Bake 35 to 40 minutes. While hot, poke holes in cake with skewer or ice pick. The more holes the better. Into holes pour mixture of confectioner's sugar and 4 tablespoons pineapple juice. Let soak in well. Cool 2 to 3 hours.

OLD-FASHIONED FRUITCAKE, LIGHT

1 lb. butter	½ lb. raisins
2 cups sugar	1 lb. currants
6 eggs	½ lb. chopped citron
4 cups flour	½ lb. mixed candied fruit
¼ tsp. nutmeg	½ lb. chopped almonds
¼ cup molasses	¼ cup bourbon

Preheat oven to 250° F.

Line 10 × 6 × 2-inch pan with paper.

Cream butter and sugar until light and fluffy. Add eggs one at a time and beat well after each addition. Add nutmeg, molasses, nuts, and fruit (that have been rolled in extra flour). Sift flour, add to mixture. Last, add bourbon and mix thoroughly. Place in prepared pan and bake for 4 hours.

ECONOMY ANGEL FOOD CAKE

1½ cups sugar	1 tsp. vanilla
4 Tbs. water	1 cup flour
8 or 9 egg whites (1 cup)	¼ tsp. salt
1 tsp. cream of tartar	

Preheat oven to 325° F.

Grease and flour 10-inch tube pan.

Boil sugar and water together until mixture balls when dropped into cold water.

Beat egg whites and cream of tartar until stiff and pour sugar water into whites, beating all the time. Add vanilla and beat until cool. Sift flour and salt, and gradually fold into egg mixture. Pour into prepared pan and bake for about 50 minutes.

SPONGE CAKE

8 eggs, separated
1½ cups sugar
1 whole egg
1¾ cups flour

½ tsp. lemon or orange or vanilla flavoring (to taste)

Preheat oven to 300° F.

Grease and sugar (use granulated sugar) a 10-inch tube pan.

Mix egg yolks and sugar together. Beat until thick and creamy. Add one whole egg and continue beating until sugar is dissolved and light and fluffy.

Measure and sift flour. Add to egg mixture in three parts, each time using a spatula to fold in. Add flavoring. Beat egg whites until stiff and—very gently—fold into the batter. Pour into prepared pan and bake for 45 to 50 minutes.

4

Frostings, Icings, and Sauces

VERY OFTEN the terms "frosting" and "icing" are used interchangeably. In fact, there is a difference. A frosting is richer and more substantial and is usually made with butter or cream cheese and sometimes eggs. It is generally cooked or otherwise heated (over water in the top of a double boiler). It is usually put on a cooled cake. Frostings are sometimes uncooked and are quite delicious. They may be used as a filling between layers as well as on top or sides.

Icings are of a thinner consistency than frostings. They are made with confectioner's sugar and are usually not cooked, although some cooks mix the icing and stir it over low heat for a few minutes to take away the raw taste. A recipe using two cups of sugar will cover the entire top and middle of an 8- or 9-inch 2-layer cake.

MY OWN CHOCOLATE FUDGE FROSTING

½ cup milk
2½ cups confectioner's sugar
4 squares unsweetened
    chocolate

3 Tbs. butter
1 tsp. vanilla

Put milk, sugar, and chocolate together in saucepan. Add butter. Let come to a boil. Continue to boil slowly for about 5 minutes. Add vanilla. Beat about 10 times. (Do not over-beat or it will harden.) Frost cooled cake immediately. Enough for three 9-inch layers or one 13 × 9 × 2-inch sheet cake.

HUNGARIAN CHOCOLATE FROSTING

4 to 5 squares unsweetened
    chocolate
2¼ cups sifted confectioner's
    sugar

¼ cup hot water
2 egg yolks, beaten
6 Tbs. butter
1 tsp. vanilla

Melt chocolate and remove from heat. Add sugar and water and blend. Add yolks, one at a time, beating after each. Add butter, a tablespoon at a time, beating thoroughly after each addition. Add vanilla. Enough frosting for top and sides of two 9-inch layers or 13 × 9 × 2-inch sheet cake.

CHOCOLATE WHIP

⅓ cup cocoa
1½ cups heavy cream

½ cup sugar

Add cocoa and sugar to heavy cream. Let stand 1 hour in refrigerator; beat stiff.

Variation

Add ¼ cup chocolate syrup to 1½ cups heavy cream, whipped.

CHOCOLATE DREAM FROSTING

3 squares unsweetened
    chocolate
1 (3-oz.) package cream
    cheese

¼ cup milk
Dash of salt
3½ cups sifted confectioner's
    sugar

Melt chocolate over hot water. Soften cream cheese with about 1 tablespoon of milk. Add salt and sugar alternately with remaining milk, blending well. Add chocolate and beat until smooth and of spreading consistency. Will cover top and sides of two 10-inch or three 9-inch layers, or one 13 × 9 × 2-inch loaf.

COCONUT-PECAN FROSTING

1 cup evaporated milk
1 cup sugar
3 egg yolks
½ cup butter

1 tsp. vanilla
1⅓ cups flaked coconut
1 cup chopped pecans

Combine in saucepan milk, sugar, yolks, butter, and vanilla. Cook over medium heat, stirring constantly for about 12 minutes or until thickened. Remove from heat and add coconut and pecans. Beat until cool and of spreading consistency. Will cover tops of three 9-inch layers.

PINEAPPLE CREAM FROSTING

½ cup butter
4 cups sifted confectioner's
    sugar

6 Tbs. crushed pineapple
1 to 2 Tbs. pineapple juice
Pineapple slices

Cream butter and sugar together. Stir in well-drained, crushed pineapple and juice. Beat thoroughly. Spread on top and sides of cake. Decorate with ½ pineapple slices. Will cover sides, top, and fill two 10-inch layers, or three 9-inch layers.

FLUFFY SEVEN-MINUTE FROSTING

2 egg whites, unbeaten   Dash of salt
1½ cups light corn syrup   1 tsp. vanilla

Combine egg whites, syrup, and salt in top of double boiler, beating with rotary egg beater until thoroughly mixed. Place over rapidly boiling water and continue beating constantly for 7 minutes, or until frosting stands in peaks. Using electric mixer to beat cuts time in half. Add vanilla and beat until thick enough to spread. Enough for two 10-inch or three 9-inch layers.

PECAN CREAM FROSTING

3 Tbs. soft butter   1 tsp. vanilla
2 cups confectioner's sugar   ½ cup pecans
4 Tbs. cream

Beat butter with confectioner's sugar. Add cream, vanilla, and pecans. Will fill and frost two 9-inch layers.

RICH CHOCOLATE BUTTER-CREAM FROSTING

2 cups confectioner's sugar   4 Tbs. cream
4 Tbs. soft butter   1 tsp. vanilla
1 cup cocoa

Cream butter and sugar. Add cocoa and cream to butter mixture. Add vanilla last. Beat until of spreading consistency. Smooth on cake with spatula. Will fill and frost two 9-inch layers.

Variation

Substitute strong coffee for the cream to give a mocha taste.

ORANGE FROSTING

⅓ cup butter or whipped margarine
3 cups confectioner's sugar

3 Tbs. orange juice
1½ Tbs. fresh grated orange rind

Blend butter and sugar. Add juice and rind. Will fill and cover two 8-inch layers.

CHOCOLATE SATIN FROSTING

2 Tbs. water
1 Tb. butter
¼ tsp. vanilla
1 square unsweetened chocolate

1 cup sifted confectioner's sugar

Heat water, butter, and chocolate until melted. Add vanilla. Add sifted sugar. Beat until of spreading consistency. Will frost top and center of two 9-inch layers.

CARAMEL SAUCE

1 Tb. butter
1 pound brown sugar
2 egg yolks
1 cup heavy cream

⅛ tsp. salt
1 Tb. vanilla
Slivered almonds

Mix all the ingredients except the nuts. Cook in top of double boiler until smooth and creamy. Add a handful of slivered almonds and serve with Coconut Mousse, custard, or ice cream.

CHOCOLATE SAUCE

½ package (4-oz.) semisweet chocolate
6 Tbs. water

¼ cup sugar
2 Tbs. butter

Combine chocolate and water in saucepan. Place over

low heat and stir until smooth. Add sugar and stir until dissolved. Boil gently for four minutes, stirring constantly. Remove from heat; add butter and blend. Serve hot with Torte, ice cream, or custards.

RASPBERRY MELBA SAUCE

1½ tsps. cornstarch
½ cup currant jelly

1 package (10-oz.) frozen raspberries, thawed

Blend cornstarch with 1 tablespoon juice from raspberries to make smooth paste. Set aside. In 1-quart saucepan heat jelly with raspberries. Stir in cornstarch mixture. Cook, stirring constantly, until thick and clear. Cool. Serve with poached peaches, custard, or ice cream.

APRICOT MARMALADE SAUCE

1 cup apricot preserves
1 cup orange marmalade
Juice of 2 large oranges

2 Tbs. lemon juice
4 Tbs. slivered, blanched almonds

Over low heat melt preserves and marmalade. Stir in orange juice, lemon juice and mix well. Add more lemon juice to taste, if desired. Before serving, add slivered almonds. Serve with ice cream, sponge cake, or angel food cake.

HARD SAUCE

½ cup sweet butter
1½ cups confectioner's sugar

2 Tbs. brandy, rum, or liqueur

Cream butter until light, then beat in confectioner's sugar and brandy, rum, or liqueur. In an electric mixer this takes but one minute. Chill before serving. Wonderful with plum pudding, Apple Betty and fruit charlottes.

APRICOT SAUCE

½ pound dried apricots ½ cup sugar

Soak apricots for 2 hours in enough water to cover. Boil in same water and after it boils put the apricots and liquid in which they were cooked into electric blender, if you have one, and purée; otherwise, put through sieve. Cook until sugar is dissolved. If the sauce is too thick add hot water.

VANILLA SAUCE

1 cup milk
1 cup cream
½ tsp. vanilla
4 egg yolks

½ cup sugar
¼ cup heavy cream, whipped
    (optional)

Scald milk and cream. Add vanilla. Beat egg yolks with sugar and combine with the milk and cream, stirring with a whisk. Cook in top of double boiler, stirring constantly until it coats spoon. If you wish a richer sauce fold in ¼ cup whipped cream after cooking. Serve with bread pudding.

LEMON SAUCE

1 cup sugar
2 Tbs. cornstarch
2 cups boiling water

1 lemon rind, grated
Juice of 1 lemon
2 Tbs. butter

Mix sugar and cornstarch in saucepan. Add boiling water gradually, stirring constantly. Cook 10 minutes. Add lemon rind, juice, and butter. Cook 1 minute more. Serve either hot or cold, on gingerbread.

SABAYON SAUCE I

⅔ cup sugar
4 egg yolks

1 cup white wine
Rum to taste

Beat sugar with egg yolks until light and stir in white

wine. Put in top of double boiler over cold water. Cook until water in boiler reaches boiling. Add rum to taste. Serve on poached fruits.

SABAYON SAUCE II

2 eggs
¾ cup sugar
1 cup sherry, port, or
    Madeira wine

1 small lemon, sliced
1 stick cinnamon

Beat eggs and sugar until light. Heat wine to boiling point and pour over eggs, beating all the time. Add lemon slices and cinnamon and cook over hot water in top of double boiler until thick. Remove lemon slices. Serve immediately.

ENGLISH SAUCE

6 Tbs. sugar
1 Tb. cornstarch
1 pt. milk
2 Tbs. butter or margarine

6 egg yolks
1½ tsps. vanilla extract
½ cup heavy cream

In medium saucepan combine sugar and cornstarch. Gradually add milk, stirring until smooth. Add butter and cook over medium heat, stirring constantly, until mixture thickens and comes to a boil. Boil 1 minute. Remove from heat. In medium bowl slightly beat yolks; gradually add a little hot mixture; blend well. Stir into rest of hot milk mixture. Cook over medium heat, stirring constantly, just until mixture boils. Remove from heat; stir in vanilla. Strain custard immediately into bowl; place sheet of wax paper directly on surface so skin won't form. Refrigerate until cool. Stir in heavy cream. Return to refrigerator until well chilled. Serve with Venezuelan Esponjoso (p. 100).

STRAWBERRY SAUCE

1 qt. fresh strawberries or 3 (10 oz. each) packages frozen sliced strawberries	¾ Tb. Grand Marnier Sugar to taste

Put fresh strawberries, washed, hulled, and halved, or frozen sliced (thawed) strawberries, in a small saucepan with sugar to taste. Heat until strawberries are hot but not mushy. Remove from heat and stir in Grand Marnier. Serve sauce warm, on ice cream or fresh raspberries.

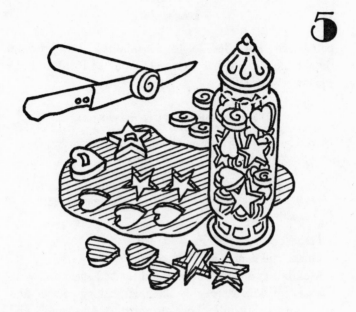

5

Small Cakes and Cookies

BEA'S FUDGEY BROWNIES

2 squares unsweetened
   chocolate
½ cup butter
1 cup sugar
2 eggs, separated

¼ tsp. salt
½ cup flour
½ tsp. vanilla
½ cup walnuts or pecans

Preheat oven to 350° F.

Grease and flour 8- or 9-inch square pan.

Melt chocolate and butter together. Add sugar. Beat yolks and fold in stiffly beaten egg whites very gently. Set aside. Add salt, vanilla, and flour to the chocolate mixture and mix well. Very carefully fold egg mixture into the chocolate batter. Fold in walnuts or pecans. Place into prepared pan. Bake for 15 to 20 minutes. The brownies should look moist but not wet. Cool and cut into 18 squares.

TAKE-THE-CAKE BROWNIES

⅓ cup butter
2 squares unsweetened
     chocolate
1 cup sugar
2 eggs
⅔ cup sifted flour

½ tsp. baking powder
¼ tsp. salt
1 tsp. vanilla
½ cup walnuts or pecans
Confectioner's sugar

Preheat oven to 350° F.

Grease and flour 8- or 9-inch square pan.

Melt butter and chocolate together. Add sugar and well-beaten eggs. Mix thoroughly. Sift flour, baking powder, and salt together. Stir into chocolate mixture. Add vanilla and nuts. Pour into prepared pan. Bake for 35 minutes. Cool and cut into 18 squares. Sift confectioner's sugar over the cooled brownies.

CRUNCHY CHOCOLATE BALLS

3 cups corn flakes
1 cup semisweet chocolate
     bits
2 cups sifted flour
¼ tsp. baking soda
½ tsp. salt
1 cup soft butter

½ cup chopped nutmeats
½ cup brown sugar
½ cup granulated sugar
1 tsp. rum flavoring
1 egg
¼ cup sifted confectioner's
     sugar

Preheat oven to 350° F.

Crush corn flakes into fine crumbs (should make ¾ cup). Chop chocolate into fine pieces. Sift flour, soda, and salt together. Mix with corn-flake crumbs and half the chocolate. Blend butter, sugars, and flavoring until light and fluffy. Add egg and beat well. Add mixed dry ingredients, stirring until combined. Drop in rounded teaspoonfuls onto ungreased baking sheet. Bake about 12 minutes. Combine remaining chopped chocolate and confectioner's sugar and nutmeats. As hot cookies are removed from baking sheets, dip tops in the mixture.   MAKES 3 DOZEN

X   QUEEN ANNE'S LACE COOKIES

½ cup granulated sugar   1 tsp. baking powder
½ cup brown sugar   1 beaten egg
 1 stick of butter   1 cup uncooked oatmeal
½ tsp. salt   1 tsp. vanilla

Preheat oven to 350° F.

Grease and flour cookie sheet.

Put sugars into bowl. Melt butter and mix with sugar. Mix in salt and baking powder, the beaten egg. Last, fold in oatmeal and vanilla. Mix and let stand until firm. Drop from teaspoon 3 inches apart on prepared sheet. Bake for 8 to 10 minutes. Let stand for one minute, no more, and remove from pan.   MAKES ABOUT 3 DOZEN

TANGERETTES

6 Tbs. sugar   2 egg whites, beaten stiff
2 Tbs. flour   Shredded peel of 2
6 oz. almonds, chopped   tangerines

Preheat oven to 350° F.

Butter cookie sheet.

Mix sugar, flour, and almonds. Fold in stiffly beaten egg whites and, last, tangerine peel. Drop batter in small balls 2 inches apart on cookie sheet. Bake for 5 minutes. Increase heat to 400° F. and bake 10 minutes longer. Remove while warm.   MAKES ABOUT 1 DOZEN

APRICOCROONS

2 cups confectioner's sugar
½ cup flour
½ tsp. baking powder
½ cup egg whites
1 cup cut-up dried apricots

½ cup pecans, walnuts, or
    toasted almonds
1 cup shredded or flaked
    coconut

Preheat oven to 325° F.

Combine sugar, flour, baking powder, and egg whites in bowl. Mix well. Add apricots, nuts, and coconut. Stir into mixture. Drop from a teaspoon onto a greased cookie sheet, 3 inches apart. Bake for about 15 minutes.

FLORENTINES I

½ cup cream
3 Tbs. butter
½ cup sugar
1¼ cups chopped almonds
⅓ cup sifted flour

¾ cup chopped candied
    orange peel
Melted sweet chocolate
    (enough to cover
    cookies)

Preheat oven to 350° F.

Grease baking sheet.

In saucepan put cream, butter, and sugar and boil. Remove from heat and stir in almonds, flour, and orange peel. From tablespoon drop batter 3 inches apart onto baking sheet. Bake for 10 minutes. Cool for five minutes and remove immediately to cake rack. With spatula spread chocolate on smooth side of cookies.

FLORENTINES II

½ cup sugar
⅓ cup heavy cream
⅓ cup honey
2 Tbs. butter
¼ cup candied orange peel,
    finely chopped

1 cup sliced almonds
3 Tbs. sifted flour
8 oz. semisweet chocolate
1 Tb. butter

Preheat oven to 400° F.

Grease baking sheet very well.

Combine sugar, cream, honey, butter in a saucepan. Stir over low heat until sugar is dissolved. Raise heat and boil without stirring until mixture forms ball when dropped into cold water. Cool slightly. Stir in orange peel, nuts, and flour. (If you have a blender, the orange peel is easily chopped at medium speed for 1 minute.)

Drop small teaspoonfuls of batter 3 inches apart on prepared pan. Flatten each with a fork or a glass dipped in milk. Cookies will spread in baking. Bake 8 to 10 minutes or until brown. Working very quickly, remove from oven and put on plate to cool. If they lose their shape upon removing, press with a glass. If they start to stick to the pan as they cool, put back in the oven for a few seconds so that they will handle more easily.

Melt semisweet chocolate and stir in butter. Coat bottom of the cookies with melted chocolate and put in refrigerator just long enough to set.   MAKES ABOUT 3 DOZEN

DATE AND NUT FINGERS

¼ cup butter	2 eggs, well beaten
1 cup sugar	1 cup dates, cut fine
¾ cup flour	1 cup pecans or walnuts,
¼ tsp. baking powder	chopped
Pinch salt	Confectioner's sugar

Preheat oven to 350° F.

Line an 8- or 9-inch square pan with wax paper.

Cream butter and sugar until light. Sift flour, baking powder, and salt. Add eggs to butter and sugar mixture. Then add flour mixture. Fold in dates and nuts. Spread in prepared pan. Bake for 15 to 20 minutes. Cut into "fingers," that is, narrow bars. Roll in confectioner's sugar while warm.

RAISIN DOMINO COOKIES

¼ cup soft butter
1 cup light brown sugar,
     packed
1 egg
1 tsp. vanilla
¼ tsp. almond extract

¾ cup sifted flour
½ tsp. baking powder
½ tsp. salt
¾ cup chopped raisins
⅓ cup chopped pecans

Preheat oven to 350° F.

Grease 9-inch square pan and flour it.

Blend butter, brown sugar, egg, vanilla, and almond extract until smooth. Blend in flour, resifted with baking
powder and salt. Mix in raisins and pecans. Spread in prepared pan. Bake about 25 minutes. Cool in pan. Frost with
following icing:

Icing

1½ cups sifted confectioner's
     sugar
1 Tbs. soft butter

½ tsp. vanilla
1½ Tbs. milk
Raisins for decoration

Combine sugar, butter, vanilla, and milk. If necessary
add a few more drops of milk to make spreadable. Frost
cookies. Cut them into 9 × 1-inch bars. Decorate with
raisins to represent markings of dominos.

DREAM BARS

½ cup butter
½ cup brown sugar
1 cup flour
2 eggs
1 cup brown sugar
1 tsp. vanilla

2 Tbs. flour
½ tsp. baking powder
¼ tsp. salt
1½ cups coconut
1 cup walnuts or pecans,
     chopped

Preheat oven to 325° F.

Cream butter and ½ cup brown sugar and beat well.
Blend in 1 cup flour. Spread mixture on greased jelly-roll
pan. Bake for 15 minutes. Meanwhile, beat eggs and add 1
cup brown sugar and vanilla. Add 2 tablespoons flour, bak-

ing powder, salt. Add coconut and nuts. Spread over baked mixture and return to oven for 25 minutes. Cool before taking from the pan.

JIMBLE JUMBLES

¼ pound butter
1 cup (6-oz. package) semi-sweet chocolate morsels
1 package (10-oz.) miniature marshmallows
1 package (8- or 10-oz.) rice cereal

2 cups Spanish peanuts
1 or 2 cups chopped pecans
1 cup raisins
3 cups popped popcorn

Melt butter, chocolate, and marshmallows together in top of double boiler. Mix remaining ingredients in a very large bowl. Pour melted chocolate mixture over dry ingredients and mix thoroughly. Then spoon the mixture into half-gallon paper milk carton. Pack tightly and place in refrigerator. In about 2 hours the jimble jumble will be ready to serve. Peel away the carton and with very sharp knife cut jumble into either squares or fingers.　Serves 8

CHOCOLATE ALMOND CRISPS

1 cup butter
1 cup sifted confectioner's sugar
2 egg yolks
1 tsp. vanilla
2 cups sifted flour

¼ tsp. salt
1 cup toasted diced almonds
1 package (6-oz.) semisweet chocolate pieces
1 cup sifted confectioner's sugar

Preheat oven to 375° F.

Beat butter and 1 cup of the sugar until light and fluffy. Beat egg yolks and vanilla. Add rest of the ingredients, except remaining cup of sugar, and stir until mixed well. Drop by teaspoonfuls onto well greased cookie sheet. Bake for 10 minutes or until golden in color. Sprinkle remaining sugar over the still-warm cookies.

THE-GANG'S-ALL-HERE BROWNIES
When you wish to serve a large group,
here is an excellent cake-type brownie recipe

3 sticks of butter
6 squares unsweetened chocolate
6 eggs
3 cups sugar
2¼ cups sifted flour
¾ tsp. baking powder
¼ tsp. salt
1 tsp. vanilla
1 cup chopped pecans or walnuts

Preheat oven to 350° F.

Grease well and flour 9 × 13 × 2-inch pan.

Melt butter and chocolate in top of double boiler. Add eggs, one at a time, beating well after each addition. Add sugar. Sift flour, baking powder, and salt. Stir gently into chocolate mixture. Add vanilla and nuts. Pour into prepared pan. Bake for 20 minutes. Cool and cut into fingers or bars. Sprinkle with sifted confectioner's sugar.

MAKES ABOUT 2 DOZEN

DOUBLE CRUNCHERS

1 cup sifted flour
½ tsp. baking soda
¼ tsp. salt
½ cup butter
½ cup granulated sugar
½ cup brown sugar
1 egg
½ tsp. vanilla
1 cup corn flakes, crushed
1 cup quick-cooking rolled oats
½ cup coconut

Preheat oven to 350° F.

Sift flour, soda, and salt together. Set aside. Combine butter and sugars and beat until light and fluffy. Blend in egg and vanilla. Stir in flour mixture. Add corn flakes, oats, and coconut. Remove ⅓ of the dough and reserve. Shape the remaining ⅔ of the dough into small balls using level teaspoonful for each, and place on greased cookie sheet.

Flatten with bottom of a glass dipped in flour. Bake for 8 to 10 minutes.

Shape reserved dough into balls using ½ teaspoon as measure of size. Bake on greased cookie sheets for 8 to 10 minutes. Cool. Spread chocolate filling over larger cookie and top with small one.

Chocolate Filling

1 package (6-oz.) semisweet chocolate	½ cup confectioner's sugar
1 Tb. water	3 oz. cream cheese

Melt semisweet chocolate pieces with confectioner's sugar and water. Blend in cream cheese. Beat until smooth.

MAKES 2 TO 3 DOZEN

KOURAMBIEDES
A Greek melt-in-your-mouth cookie

1 lb. sweet butter	¾ cup finely chopped almonds
¼ cup confectioner's sugar	Additional confectioner's sugar
1 egg yolk	
6 cups flour	

Preheat oven to 375° F.

Melt butter, bring to a boil and stir occasionally. Remove and turn slowly into mixing bowl. Add the sugar and yolk and beat for 2 minutes. Add the flour gradually, mixing constantly. Knead vigorously for about 30 minutes. At this point the dough is crumbly, but smooth. Add the nuts and knead thoroughly for about 10 more minutes. Pinch off small amounts of dough and form into ¾-inch balls. Place on cookie sheet ¾-inch apart. Bake about 30 to 40 minutes. Cool. Sift sugar into large bowl and roll cookies in it. These will keep 2 weeks in a tightly covered container.

YIELD: 4 DOZEN

SEQUOIA BROWNIES

½ lb. butter
4 squares unsweetened
   chocolate
2 lbs. dark brown sugar
1 cup flour

½ tsp. salt
4 eggs
1 Tb. vanilla extract
2 cups chopped walnuts
30 walnut halves

DO NOT PREHEAT OVEN!

Line a 1-inch deep cookie pan with wax paper.

Melt the butter, chocolate, and sugar in top of double boiler over hot water. Remove from heat and stir in the flour and salt. Add the eggs one at a time, beating well between each addition. Stir in remaining ingredients. Pour brownie mixture into prepared pan. Dot with walnut halves. Place in oven; turn oven to 300° F. and bake for 45 minutes. Turn heat off and let pan stand in oven for another 15 minutes. Remove and invert pan on flat surface. Peel off wax paper. Let cool about 1 hour and cut into squares.

YIELD: 80 TO 90 BROWNIES

MOLASSES BUTTER-RUM BALLS

1 cup butter
¼ cup molasses
2 Tbs. granulated sugar
2 cups flour
½ tsp. salt

1 cup finely chopped pecans
   or walnuts
1 cup chopped coconut
1½ tsps. rum flavoring
   Confectioner's sugar

Preheat oven to 350° F.

Grease cookie sheet.

Cream butter with molasses and sugar. Sift flour with salt; stir in nuts and coconut. Combine two mixtures and blend thoroughly. Blend in rum flavoring. Chill dough an hour or so, then shape teaspoonfuls of dough into small balls. Place on cookie sheet and bake for 18 to 20 minutes. Roll in confectioner's sugar while still warm.

YIELD: ABOUT 4 DOZEN

BUTTERSCOTCH COFFEE SPICE BARS

1 cup firmly packed brown
    sugar
½ cup soft shortening
1 egg
½ cup hot water
1 tsp. instant coffee powder
1½ cups sifted flour

1 tsp. baking powder
½ tsp. baking soda
½ tsp. salt
½ tsp. cinnamon
1 package (6-oz.) butter-
    scotch morsels
½ cup chopped nuts

Preheat oven to 350° F.

Grease and flour 13 × 9 × 2-inch pan.

Combine sugar, shortening and egg; beat until creamy. Combine hot water and coffee. Blend into creamed mixture. Sift together the flour, baking powder, soda, salt, and cinnamon. Stir gradually into creamed mixture. Add butterscotch morsels and chopped nuts. Spread in prepared pan. Bake 20 to 25 minutes. Cut into 3″ × 1½″ bars.

YIELD: 2 DOZEN

BLENDER VIENNESE COOKIES

1 cup pecans
2½ cups sifted flour
1 cup semisweet chocolate
    chips
4 eggs
1 cup soft butter

1 cup light brown sugar
2 pieces thin lemon rind,
    1 × 2 inches
1 tsp. salt
½ tsp. cloves
½ tsp. cinnamon

Preheat oven to 400° F.

Chop pecans fine, in blender, chopping half cup at a time. Add flour and chocolate chips to pecans in large mixing bowl. Put remaining ingredients into blender, cover and process until blended. Pour into flour mixture and mix well. Drop by teaspoonfuls, 2 inches apart, onto ungreased cookie sheet. Bake 6 to 8 minutes until lightly browned.

YIELD: 7 DOZEN

COCONUT CRUNCH

¾ cup butter
3 cups brown sugar
1⅔ cups flour
1 tsp. salt
1 Tb. baking powder

3 eggs, unbeaten
1½ tsp. vanilla
1 cup coconut
1 cup chopped pecans

Preheat oven to 350° F.

Grease 9 × 12 × 2-inch pan.

Melt butter, stir in brown sugar. Sift flour, salt, and baking powder together, and add to sugar mixture. Add eggs one at a time, beating well after each addition. Blend in vanilla, coconut, and pecans. Pour into prepared pan. Bake for about 40 minutes. Cut into squares when cooled.

YIELD: 1 TO 2 DOZEN

✗ HOLIDAY FRUITED COOKIES

½ cup soft shortening
1¼ cups dark brown sugar, firmly packed
1 tsp. salt
1 egg
1¾ cups sifted flour
½ tsp. cinnamon
1 tsp. ground cloves
⅛ tsp. nutmeg

1 tsp. baking soda
1 cup canned applesauce
½ cup walnuts, chopped
½ cup filberts, chopped
¾ cup chopped dates
¼ cup chopped prunes
½ cup chopped mixed candied fruit
Confectioner's sugar icing

Preheat oven to 400° F.

Grease baking sheets.

In mixing bowl combine shortening, brown sugar, salt, and egg. Beat thoroughly until well blended. Sift together flour, cinnamon, cloves, nutmeg and soda. Add ½ of flour mixture to shortening mix. Blend well. Stir in applesauce, nuts, and fruits. Add remaining flour. Blend well. Drop by rounded tablespoonfuls 3 inches apart on baking sheets. Bake for 12 to 15 minutes. Remove cookies from baking sheet and cool on wire rack. Frost with confectioner's sugar icing.

Confectioner's Sugar Icing

1 cup confectioner's sugar ⅛ tsp. salt
1 Tb. butter 1 Tb. milk, scalded

Beat all ingredients together until creamy.

YIELD: 3½ DOZEN

COCOA PEANUT LOGS
Easy for children to make. No baking

1 cup semisweet chocolate 4 cups cocoa-flavored corn
  pieces puffs
⅓ cup peanut butter

Butter a 9 × 9 × 2-inch pan or comparable-sized rectangular pan.

Melt chocolate with peanut butter in heavy medium-sized saucepan over low heat, stirring constantly until well blended. Remove from heat. Add cocoa corn puffs, stirring until coated with chocolate mixture. Press mixture into prepared pan. Let stand in cool place or refrigerate until hardened. Cut into log-shaped bars.

YIELD: 1½ DOZEN

6

Coffee Cakes and Buns

COFFEE CAKES

In the 1600's, there appeared on the Polish scene a yeast coffee cake which was called *Babka*. At the same time the Austro-Hungarian Empire created the *Gugelhopf* or as it became known, the *Kugelhof*, also variously spelled: *Gougelhof; Gugelhupf*. King Stanislaus of Poland lost his throne in 1766 when Poland was partitioned and he promptly set up in a magnificent chateau in the suburbs of Paris. There he indulged in his favorite pastime—cooking. One day he took *kugelhof* dough, poured it into molds and, when the cakes were baked, soaked them while still warm with hot rum. He called this sensational concoction Ali Baba after his favorite storybook character.

When this delight traveled to France, it was called only *baba*, or as it is known today, *baba au rhum*. In France, the master chef, Julien, used the same dough, changed its shape, added his own refinements and called it *Savarin* in honor of the great Brillat-Savarin. The Russians also have a similar coffee cake, which they call *kulich*.

Baking Powder Coffee Cakes

CLAIRE'S COFFEE CAKE

½ pound butter	Pinch salt
¾ cup sugar	½ tsp. baking soda
5 eggs	1 cup sour cream
2¾ cups flour	2 tsps. vanilla
2 tsps. baking powder	Cinnamon mixture

Preheat oven to 350° F.

Butter 10-inch tube pan.

Cream butter with sugar until light and fluffy. Add eggs, unseparated, one at a time and beat in. Sift flour, baking powder, salt, and soda together. Beat in sour cream with creamed mixture and carefully stir in flour mixture. Add vanilla. Put ½ of batter in prepared pan. Sprinkle with mixture of sugar, cinnamon, and chopped nuts. Add rest of batter and sprinkle rest of cinnamon mixture on top. Bake for 40 minutes.

Cinnamon mixture

¼ cup sugar	½ cup chopped nuts
2 tsps. cinnamon	

P. M. PECAN COFFEE CAKE

2 tsps. baking powder
½ tsp. salt
1½ cups sifted flour
2 eggs, separated
½ cup milk
½ tsp. vanilla

⅓ cup butter
⅔ cup sugar
¾ cup chopped pecans
¼ cup sugar
½ tsp. cinnamon
2 Tbs. butter

Preheat oven to 375° F.

Grease well and flour a 9 × 9 × 2-inch square pan.

Sift together baking powder, salt, and flour. Beat egg yolks with milk and vanilla. Cream butter with ⅔ cup sugar. Alternately add liquid and dry ingredients to butter mixture, stirring well after each addition. Fold in stiffly beaten egg whites. Pour batter into prepared pan. Sprinkle pecans, ¼ cup of sugar, and ½ teaspoon cinnamon over the batter in the pan. Dot with butter and bake for 30 minutes. Cut into squares and serve warm.

RAISIN BROWN SUGAR ROLLS

⅔ cup seedless raisins
2 cups sifted all purpose flour
¼ cup granulated sugar
4 tsps. baking powder
1 tsp. salt
⅓ cup butter

⅔ cup milk
2 Tbs. melted butter
1 tsp. cinnamon
½ cup brown sugar
1 Tb. corn syrup

Preheat oven to 375° F.

Grease an 8-inch square pan with 1 tablespoon butter.

Rinse raisins and drain. Sift together flour, sugar, baking powder, and salt. Cut in ⅓ cup butter. Add raisins and milk and mix well. Roll out to rectangle (about 9 × 15 inches). Spread with 1 tablespoon melted butter and sprinkle with cinnamon. Roll from long side, as for jelly roll. Cut into 9 one-inch slices. Combine brown sugar and corn syrup and spread over butter in pan. Place rolls flat in sugar. Bake about 25 minutes. Turn out sugar side up.

EYE-OPENER PRUNE COFFEE CAKE

2 cups flour
1 tsp. baking soda
1 tsp. baking powder
Dash of salt
¼ cup butter
1 scant cup sugar

2 eggs
1 cup sour cream, room temperature
1 cup cut-up dried prunes
2 tsps. vanilla

Preheat oven to 350° F.

Grease and flour a 9 × 12 × 2-inch pan.

Sift flour, soda, baking powder, and salt together. Cream butter and sugar together until light and fluffy. Add eggs one at a time. Beat well. Fold in alternately sour cream and the flour mixture. Fold in dried prunes and vanilla. Pour into prepared pan. Bake for 30 minutes.

✗ BALTIMORE COFFEE CAKE

½ lb. butter
1 cup sugar
2 eggs
½ pint sour cream
4 Tbs. milk
2 tsps. vanilla
2½ cups flour

2 tsps. baking powder
1 tsp. baking soda
1 cup raisins
1 tsp. cinnamon
¼ cup sugar
½ cup walnuts or pecans

Preheat oven to 375° F.

Grease well 10-inch tube pan.

Cream butter and 1 cup of sugar until light and fluffy. Add eggs one at a time, beating thoroughly after each addition. Make a mixture of the sour cream, milk, and vanilla. Sift together flour, baking powder, and baking soda. Alternately add the flour mixture and the sour-cream mixture to the butter and sugar. Mix well. Add raisins. Mix ¼ cup of sugar, cinnamon, and nuts in a dish. Put half the batter into prepared pan. Sprinkle cinnamon and nuts over the batter. Add rest of the batter and sprinkle top with remaining cinnamon mixture. Bake for 35 to 40 minutes.

PARTY PRIDE COFFEE CAKE

1 cup chopped pecans	2½ cups flour
½ cup sugar	2 tsps. baking powder
1 tsp. cinnamon	1 tsp. baking soda
½ lb. butter	Pinch of salt
1 cup sugar	1 tsp. vanilla
3 eggs	1 tsp. lemon juice
1 cup sour cream	Topping

Make a mixture of the pecans, sugar, and cinnamon. Set aside.

Preheat oven to 375° F.

Grease and flour an 8-inch square cake pan.

Cream butter and 1 cup sugar until light. Add eggs one at a time, then the sour cream alternately with the sifted dry ingredients and flavoring. Pour half of batter into prepared pan and sprinkle with half of nut mixture. Add remainder of batter smoothly on top of mixture. Sprinkle with the balance of nut mixture. Sprinkle topping over cake. Bake for 40 minutes.

Topping

1 tsp. lemon juice	½ cup brown sugar
1 tsp. cinnamon	⅛ lb. butter (½ stick)
½ cup granulated sugar	

Work all together.

COCONUT BLUEBERRY COFFEE CAKE

2 cups sifted flour	1 cup milk
1 cup sugar	2 eggs, beaten
3 tsps. baking powder	1½ cups blueberries
¼ tsp. salt	1 can flaked coconut
½ cup butter, softened	

Preheat oven to 375° F.

Grease a 9 × 12 × 2-inch pan.

Sift together flour, sugar, baking powder, and salt. Cut in softened butter, using 2 knives. Mix milk and eggs together and stir into dry ingredients. Fold blueberries in gently. Pour into pan. Sprinkle coconut evenly over top of batter. Bake for 25 minutes.

BAKING POWDER QUICKIE KUCHEN DOUGH

2 cups flour	½ tsp. salt
4 tsps. baking powder	½ cup butter
2 Tbs. sugar	¾ cup milk

Preheat oven to 350° F.

Grease an 8 × 12 × 2-inch pan or a 9 × 12-inch cookie sheet.

Sift flour, baking powder, sugar, and salt. Work butter into dry ingredients. Add milk and mix quickly. Roll out onto floured board ½ inch thick and line buttered pan or cookie sheet. Top with fruit (see recipes below), sugar, and spices. Bake for 20 to 30 minutes.

APPLE KUCHEN

Kuchen dough (p. 55 and 62)	1 tsp. cinnamon
	Butter
8 apples, peeled	1 egg yolk
1 cup sugar	3 Tbs. cream
½ tsp. nutmeg	

Preheat oven to 350° F.

Cut apples into eighths and lay them in parallel rows on top of either kuchen dough. Sprinkle with sugar, nutmeg, and cinnamon. Dot with butter and bake for 10 minutes. Beat egg yolk with cream and sprinkle over apples. Continue baking 20 to 30 minutes.

IN-A-HURRY CAKE

½ cup butter
1 cup sugar
3 eggs
2 cups sifted flour
1 tsp. baking powder

½ tsp. baking soda
½ tsp. salt
1 cup sour cream
½ cup raisins
Pecan Topping

Preheat oven to 350° F.

Grease and flour a 9 × 9 × 2-inch baking pan.

Cream butter and sugar until light. Add eggs, one at a time, beating thoroughly after each addition. Add sifted dry ingredients alternately with sour cream, beating until smooth. Stir in raisins. Spread in prepared baking pan and sprinkle with Pecan Topping. Bake for 40 to 45 minutes.

Pecan Topping

¾ cup brown sugar
1 Tb. flour
1 tsp. cinnamon

2 Tbs. butter
1 cup chopped pecans

Mix ingredients together.

PRUNE KUCHEN

Kuchen dough (p. 55 or
    62)
1 qt. pitted prunes
¾ cup sugar
1 Tbs. lemon juice

1 tsp. cinnamon
2 Tbs. butter
1 egg yolk
3 Tbs. cream

Place pitted prunes upright on top of dough. Sprinkle with sugar, lemon juice, and cinnamon. Dot with butter and bake for 15 minutes at 350° F. Beat the egg yolk with cream and spread over prunes. Continue baking for about 30 minutes.

YEAST COFFEE CAKES

CHOCOLATE COFFEE CAKE

½ cup butter
¾ cup sugar
4½ cups sifted flour
2 cakes of yeast (or packages)
½ cup lukewarm or warm water
1 can (5-oz.) evaporated milk

4 egg yolks
1 package (6-oz.) semi-sweet chocolate pieces
½ tsp. vanilla
½ tsp. cinnamon
½ tsp. salt

Grease 10-inch tube pan, preferably with removable bottom.

Cream butter and sugar together until light. Divide flour in half. Dissolve yeast cakes in warm water and mix into half the flour. Fold other half of flour into creamed butter and sugar. Reserving ¼ cup evaporated milk, add water to remaining milk to make ½ cup. Add evaporated-milk mixture and egg yolks to creamed batter. Blend in remaining flour, salt and yeast mixture. Beat at medium speed for 3 minutes. Let stand in covered bowl for 1½ hours in warm place until double in bulk. Heat remaining milk until just boiling. Add chocolate pieces and cinnamon. Add vanilla. Melt, then cool. Punch down dough. Turn out onto well-floured board. Let rest a minute. Knead lightly. Roll into rectangle 10 × 15 inches. Spread with chocolate mixture. Roll up like jelly roll. Place rolled seam down in prepared pan. Seal ends. Let stand in pan in warm place for 1 hour or until double. Bake at 350° F. for 45 minutes. Carefully removed from pan while warm.

SUNDAY-GO-TO-MEETING COFFEE CAKE
Complicated but well worth the effort

5½ cups flour	1½ cups milk
1 cup sugar	3 eggs
½ tsp. salt	1 cup sour cream
¾ cup raisins	½ cup butter
2½ cakes yeast (or packages)	

Sift 5 cups flour (reserving ½ cup), sugar, and salt together. Mix dry ingredients and raisins. Dissolve yeast in ½ cup of warm milk and add remaining flour. Make hole in center of sifted dry ingredients and pour in yeast mixture. Mix gently. In another bowl mix eggs and sour cream together and beat well. Melt butter in remaining milk. Add to sour-cream mixture. After foamy yeast sponge has formed, add all liquids to flour mixture. Put in refrigerator in the evening, covered with aluminum foil paper and a plate.

In the morning preheat oven to 350° F.

Butter two 9 × 5-inch loaf pans.

Stir down the dough and place in prepared pans. Let rise in warm place for 1 hour. Top with Streusel. Bake at 350° F. for 35 to 45 minutes.

Streusel

1 tsp. cinnamon	4 Tbs. sugar
3 Tbs. flour	2 Tbs. butter

Combine.

HOCUS-POCUS BUNS

1 package yeast	½ cup butter
¼ cup warm water	3¾ cups flour
½ cup lukewarm milk	24 large marshmallows
¼ cup sugar	1 cup butter, melted
¼ tsp. salt	1 Tb. cinnamon
1 egg	1 cup sugar

Grease 12 large-sized muffin tins.

Dissolve yeast in water. Add milk, ¼ cup sugar, salt, egg, ½ cup butter, and half the flour. Mix with spoon until smooth. Add enough of the remaining flour to handle easily. Turn onto floured board and knead for 5 minutes. Cover and let rise in warm place until double for about 30 minutes. Divide dough in half. Roll out to about ¼-inch thickness. Cut twelve 3½″ circles from each half. Dip marshmallows in melted butter and cinnamon mixed with remaining sugar. Wrap dough circles around each marshmallow and pinch together. Place in prepared muffin cups pinched side down. Let rise until to top of muffin cups and bake at 350° F. for about 25 minutes.

CLASSIC KUGELHOF

1 cake yeast	½ tsp. salt
¼ cup lukewarm water	1½ Tbs. sugar
2½ cups flour	½ cup raisins
2 eggs	Confectioner's sugar
1 cup lukewarm milk	Almonds
½ cup butter	

Butter 8-inch tube pan.

Soften yeast in ¼ cup lukewarm water. Stir in about ½ cup flour and sift remaining flour over dough. Do not mix, but place bowl in warm place until soft yeast rises up through dry flour. Then mix dry flour and dough lightly and beat in eggs one at a time by hand and add the lukewarm milk. Beat for 5 minutes; add flour if needed. Cream butter, salt, and sugar until light and fluffy. Spread butter mixture over yeast mixture. Add raisins and almonds and stir through batter. Fill prepared pan half full, cover and let rise in warm place until double in bulk. Bake at 400° F. for 40 to 45 minutes. Remove from pan while still hot. When cool sprinkle with confectioner's sugar.

KUGELHOF WITH CHOCOLATE

1 recipe Classic Kugelhof	3 Tbs. milk
dough	1 tsp. vanilla
2 oz. sweet chocolate	2 Tbs. sugar

Grease and flour an 8- or 9-inch tube pan.

Make Classic Kugelhof, but add no raisins. Add enough flour so that dough is not sticky. Divide in half. Add sweet chocolate melted in milk, vanilla, and sugar to half of dough. Roll out both halves. Put the chocolate dough over the white dough. Roll up like a jelly roll and place in prepared pan. Bake at 400° F. for 10 minutes. Lower heat to 350° F. and bake for 45 minutes.

COFFEE BREAKERS

¼ cup butter	2½ cups prepared biscuit mix
⅓ cup brown sugar	2 Tbs. butter
1 tsp. corn syrup	¼ cup brown sugar ⎱combined
⅓ cup pecans	1 tsp. cinnamon ⎰
1 package or cake of yeast	
¾ cup lukewarm water	

Melt ¼ cup butter and stir in ⅓ cup brown sugar and syrup and bring to a boil. Spread immediately in bottom of greased 12 × 7 × 2-inch pan. Sprinkle with pecans.

Dissolve yeast in warm water, add to the prepared biscuit mix and beat well.

Turn dough out on a floured board. Knead until smooth. Roll into 12-inch square. Brush with 2 tablespoons of butter. Sprinkle center with half the sugar and cinnamon mixture. Fold one third over the center third. Sprinkle with remaining sugar and cinnamon. Fold remaining third over the other two. Cut with sharp knife into 1-inch strips. Take the end of each strip and twist. Seal ends firmly. Place in pan 1½ inches apart and cover. Let rise until double in bulk, about 1 hour. Bake at 400° F. for about 20 minutes. Turn out of pan immediately.

FRUIT AND NUT ROLLS

1 envelope or square of yeast	1 cup butter, melted
¼ cup lukewarm milk	2 eggs, well beaten
1 tsp. sugar	1 tsp. vanilla
½ cup hot milk	4½ cups flour
1 tsp. salt	Melted butter for brushing dough
¼ cup sugar	

Grease muffin tins or line with cupcake papers.

Dissolve yeast in lukewarm milk. Stir teaspoon sugar into yeast mixture and set aside.

In mixing bowl stir hot milk, salt, ¼ cup sugar, and melted butter until sugar is dissolved. Let mixture cool, then add yeast and eggs. Add vanilla. Beat together. Add flour, a cup at a time. Brush dough with butter, cover with clean towel, and set in warm place until it doubles (about two hours). Divide dough into 3 parts. Roll out each part. Divide Cinnamon Nut Mixture into thirds. Sprinkle each section with mixture and stack sections. Roll up like jelly roll and slice in ½ inch slices. Bake at 375° F. for 20 minutes.

Cinnamon Nut Mixture

¼ cup sugar	½ cup raisins
2 tsps. cinnamon	½ cup walnuts

Combine.

OH, SO PEACHY COFFEE CAKE

½ lb. butter	3 cups flour
¾ cup sugar	6 fresh peach halves
1 cup flour	¼ cup butter
½ tsp. salt	1 cup brown sugar
3 eggs	Sugar
½ cup sour cream	Cinnamon
½ cup light cream (or milk)	1 Tb. flour
1 cake yeast	1 Tb. melted butter
¼ cup warm water	

Cream butter with sugar, 1 cup flour, and salt. Work mixture with fingers. Make well in center and add eggs, light and sour cream. Mix well. Dissolve yeast in ¼ cup warm water. Put the yeast in a center well in dough and add the balance of the flour. Mix but do not beat. Put in covered greased bowl overnight.

Preheat oven to 375° F. Roll out on floured board ½ inch thick. DO NOT KNEAD. Cook peaches with brown sugar and butter until soft. Divide dough in 4 parts and roll each part in mixture of sugar, cinnamon, and 1 tablespoon each of flour and melted butter. Put the cooked peaches in bottom of 10-inch greased and floured tube pan. Put the 4 parts of the dough on top of peaches. Cover and let rise in warm place 1 hour. Bake 50 to 60 minutes.

RAISED KUCHEN

1 cup milk	2 eggs, lightly beaten
1 package yeast	½ tsp. salt
½ cup butter	3½ cups flour (approxi-
½ cup sugar	mately)

Line a cookie sheet with buttered brown paper.

Scald 1 cup milk and let it cool until lukewarm. Crumble 1 package or one square of yeast into the cooled milk, mixing until yeast is dissolved. Cream butter with sugar. Add eggs and salt. Add yeast mixture alternately with about 3½ cups flour, mixing thoroughly. If necessary add more flour to make a light dough. Knead until elastic. Cover with cloth and set in warm place to rise until double. Roll out ⅛ inch thick and spread on prepared cookie sheet. Bake at 350° F. for 20 to 30 minutes.

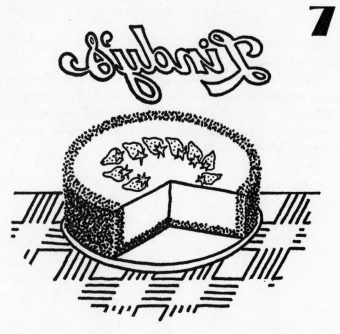

7

Cheese Cakes and Cheese Pies

CHEESE CAKE

THE GREEKS had a word for cheese cake and that word was *Tyropita*. After they got the good word, they invented cheese cake or vice versa. The Romans got the aroma of it and brought the Greek chefs to Rome to demonstrate their secret art of cheese cakery. The Romans had their own word for it. They called it *Scriblita*. The fame of the Roman cheese cake spread to Russia and France, then across the channel to England.

Through the years countless cheese cakes were created by famous chefs. The French made it into the shape of a heart and called it Coeur à la Crème. In England, sweet cheese was encased in pastry and Henry VIII called this delicacy Maids of Honour.

Finally, a couple of centuries later, cheese cake found its way to the shores of America and into New York City, where the famous restaurants Lindy's and Reubens made cheese cake a specialty of the house. In fact, it is rumored that many people think Lindy's invented it.

And so its fame spread throughout America, and in this chapter we have collected a large and varied assortment of this plebeian delicacy.

Most cheese cakes are poured into a Graham Cracker Crust (p. 79) pressed into either spring forms or pie plates.

Almost any cheese cake can be adorned with a fruit topping. Most prepared pie fillings such as cherry pie mix, blueberry pie mix, and other fruit fillings can be chilled in the refrigerator prior to use and then spread on top of almost any of the chilled cheese cakes or pies.

SOUR CREAM RHUBARB CHEESE PIE

2 packages frozen rhubarb
½ cup sugar
3 Tbs. cornstarch
4 (3-oz.) packages cream
   cheese, softened
2 eggs
½ cup sugar
1 cup sour cream
9-inch baked pie shell
Toasted almonds

Preheat oven to 425° F.

Partially thaw rhubarb. Mix ½ cup sugar and cornstarch. Add rhubarb and cook, stirring until thickened. Pour into 9-inch pie shell. Bake for 10 minutes. Beat cheese, eggs, and remaining sugar together. Pour over rhubarb. Reduce oven heat to 350° F. Return pie to oven and bake 30 minutes. Cool and spread with sour cream. Top with toasted almonds. SERVES 6 TO 8

STRAWBERRY CREAM CHEESE PIE

1 lb. cream cheese	1 cup sour cream
½ cup sugar	1 tsp. vanilla
2 well-beaten eggs	2 Tbs. sugar
2 tsps. vanilla	

Preheat oven to 350° F.

Mix first four ingredients together, using medium speed of electric mixer. Pour into graham cracker crust pressed into the bottom and sides of 9-inch pie plate (p. 79). Bake for 35 minutes.

Meanwhile blend sour cream with 1 teaspoon vanilla and 2 tablespoons of sugar. Spread on top of baked pie and return to oven (set at 425° F.) for 5 minutes. Cool and add Strawberry Crown.

Strawberry Crown

1 pt. fresh strawberries	1½ tsps. cornstarch
3 Tbs. water	1 Tb. cold water
¼ cup sugar	

Select a number of the most perfect strawberries and arrange on top of the cooled pie. Crush remaining berries and put into small saucepan with 3 tablespoons of water and sugar. Simmer 10 minutes and strain. Add cornstarch which has been mixed with 1 tablespoon of cold water. Cook, stirring constantly until thickened. Cook 5 minutes more, stirring constantly. Cool slightly and pour over top of pie. Let set one hour before cutting.   SERVES ABOUT 6 TO 8

KARL'S CHEESE CAKE

2¼ lbs. cream cheese	4 eggs
1½ cups sugar	2 tsps. vanilla

Preheat oven to 350° F.

Line bottom sides of 9-inch spring form with Graham Cracker Crust (p. 79). Cream the cream cheese and sugar in a mixer. Add eggs one at a time and vanilla. Beat in the mixer for ten minutes, at medium speed, loosening the mixture from the sides of the bowl while beating. Pour into spring form. Bake 20 minutes. Cool.

Topping

1 pt. sour cream   2 tsps. vanilla
4 Tbs. sugar

Mix all the ingredients together, spoon smoothly over the cake and return to the oven for five minutes at 450° F. Let cool in oven for one hour. Put in refrigerator for 24 hours. Serves 12.

SOUR CREAM CHEESE CAKE

¾ cup sugar   ½ tsp. lemon juice
3 eggs, well beaten   Grated rind of 1 lemon
3 packages (8 oz. each)   3 cups sour cream
    cream cheese   ¼ cup melted butter
1 tsp. vanilla

Preheat oven to 350° F.

Line 10-inch spring form with Graham Cracker Crust (p. 79).

Beat together sugar and eggs. Add cream cheese, vanilla, and lemon juice and rind and beat well. Beat in sour cream. Blend well and fold in melted butter. Pour into prepared spring form. Bake for 45 minutes. Chill before serving.   SERVES 10 TO 12

CHEESE PIE EXTRAORDINAIRE

6 packages (3-oz. each)
    cream cheese
1 pt. sour cream
½ cup sugar
⅛ tsp. salt

2 tsps. vanilla
2 eggs
1 Tb. lemon juice
9-inch baked pie shell

Preheat oven to 350° F.

Mix the first 7 ingredients, pour into shell and bake for 20 minutes. Cool in oven for thirty minutes. Remove and cool to room temperature. Refrigerate to chill.

SERVES 6 TO 8

CREAMY CHEESE CAKE

Crust

Bread crumbs
4 Tbs. butter
4 Tbs. sugar

4 egg yolks
2 cups flour

Sprinkle bottom of 10-inch spring form with bread crumbs.

Cream butter with sugar. Add egg yolks one at a time. Then fold in flour. Roll out on floured board and press onto bottom and sides of spring form pan and fill.

Filling

½ cup butter
½ cup sugar
4 packages (3-oz. each)
    cream cheese
½ cup cottage cheese
1 tsp. nutmeg

1 tsp. grated lemon peel
1 tsp. dry sherry
1 Tb. parmesan cheese
2 egg yolks
2 egg whites (beaten stiffly)

Preheat oven to 250° F.

Cream butter and sugar, then add cream cheese and cottage cheese and beat at low speed for about 10 minutes. Add nutmeg, lemon and sherry, parmesan cheese, and last, the egg yolks. Mix well. Fold in stiffly beaten egg whites. Pour into prepared spring form pan. Bake for 1½ hours. Let cool in oven for 1 hour. Chill in refrigerator overnight.

SERVES 10 TO 12

WHIPPED CREAM CHEESE CAKE

3 (8-oz.) containers whipped cream cheese
1 cup sugar
1 tsp. salt
¼ cup sifted flour
5 eggs, separated
¼ cup sugar

2½ Tbs. lemon juice
¼ tsp. nutmeg or mace
1 tsp. vanilla
½ tsp. almond flavoring
1 cup sour cream
Strawberry Glaze

Preheat oven to 325° F.

Line 10-inch spring form with Graham Cracker Crust (p. 79).

Combine cream cheese, 1 cup of sugar, and salt. Mix well. Add the flour and egg yolks and beat thoroughly. Mix in lemon juice, nutmeg, vanilla, almond flavoring, and sour cream. Beat egg whites until foamy, gradually adding ¼ cup sugar. Beat until stiff but not dry. Fold into cheese mixture until well blended. Pour mixture into prepared spring form. Bake for 1 hour. Cool in oven for 1 hour. Cool on rack for 30 min. and refrigerate until well chilled. Top with Strawberry Glaze.

Strawberry Glaze

1 qt. fresh strawberries
4 tsps. cornstarch
¼ cup water

½ cup sugar
1 tsp. butter

Crush enough berries to make ½ cup. Dissolve cornstarch in water. Bring berries, sugar, water and cornstarch to boil for two minutes. Stir in butter. Strain; cool. Arrange whole berries on cake. Cover with glaze. Chill.   SERVES 10 TO 12

COTTAGE CHEESE CAKE

4 eggs
1¼ cups sugar
¼ cup flour
¼ tsp. salt
2 Tbs. lemon juice
¼ tsp. lemon rind

¾ cup heavy cream
3 cups cottage cheese,
    sieved or whipped in
    blender
Preserved fruits

Preheat oven to 325° F.

Line 8-inch spring form with Graham Cracker Crust (p. 79).

Beat eggs until thick and gradually beat in sugar. Beat in flour and salt, lemon juice, rind, cream, and cottage cheese. Put into prepared spring form. Bake 1¼ hours, then cool in oven for 1 hour. Chill cake in refrigerator. Before serving, top with preserved fruit.   SERVES 8

CHOCOLATE PUDDING CHEESE CAKE

2 packages chocolate
    pudding mix
¾ cup sugar
1½ cups milk
1½ lbs. cottage cheese
4 eggs, separated

½ tsp. salt
½ pt. sour cream
1 Tb. lemon juice
1 tsp. grated lemon rind
⅓ cup flour

Preheat oven to 325° F.

Line 10-inch spring form with Graham Cracker Crust (p. 79).

Blend pudding, sugar, and milk in saucepan; cook over low heat until thick. Cool. Sieve cottage cheese. Beat egg yolks until light and blend into cheese along with remaining ingredients. Fold in stiffly beaten egg whites. Pour into prepared spring form. Bake for 1 hour and 10 minutes.

Turn off heat and let remain in oven for 30 minutes with door open. Cool to room temperature for 30 min., then chill in refrigerator. After cheese cake is chilled you may spread sour cream over top and shave semisweet chocolate over it.

LINDY'S CHEESE CAKE

Special Cookie Dough

1 cup sifted all-purpose flour	¼ tsp. vanilla
¼ cup sugar	1 egg yolk
1 tsp. grated lemon rind	¼ cup butter

Preheat oven to 550° F.

Butter 10-inch spring form pan.

Combine flour, sugar, lemon rind, and vanilla. Make well in center and add egg yolk and butter. Work mixture with hands until well blended. Chill for about 1 hour. Roll dough ¼ inch thick. Place in prepared bottom of spring-form pan. Line prepared sides with remaining dough which has been rolled and cut to fit. Fill pan with cheese mixture (recipe below). Bake for 12 minutes. Lower heat to 325° F. and bake for 1 hour. Cool in oven for 1 hour. Remove and cool 30 min. Then chill in refrigerator.

Cheese Filling

2½ lbs. cream cheese	¼ tsp. vanilla
3 Tbs. sifted flour	5 eggs
1¾ cups sugar	2 egg yolks
1½ tsps. grated orange rind	¼ cup heavy cream
1½ tsps. grated lemon rind	

Combine cheese, flour, sugar, grated rinds, and vanilla. Add eggs and egg yolks, one at a time, stirring lightly after each addition. Whip cream and fold in.　　　　SERVES 12

ROYAL MARBLE CHEESE CAKE

6 oz. of semisweet chocolate
¾ cup flour
2 Tbs. sugar
¼ tsp. salt
¼ cup butter
3 packages (8-oz.) cream
    cheese, room
    temperature

1 cup sugar
¼ cup flour
2 tsps. vanilla
1 cup sour cream
6 eggs, separated

Preheat oven to 400° F.

Make crust by melting chocolate over hot water. Combine ¾ cup flour, 2 tablespoons sugar, and salt. Cut in butter until particles are fine. Stir in 2 tablespoons chocolate. Press into prepared spring form. Bake for 10 minutes. Mix cream cheese with 1 cup sugar in mixing bowl. Blend in ¼ cup flour and vanilla extract. Add egg yolks; beat well. Blend in sour cream. Beat egg whites until soft peaks form. Fold into cheese mixture very thoroughly. Combine remaining chocolate with 1¾ cups of cheese mixture. Pour half of plain mixture over baked crust. Top with spoonfuls of half the chocolate mixture. Cover with remaining plain mixture, then with chocolate mixture. Cut through batter with spatula to marble. Place in preheated 400° F. oven. Immediately lower heat to 300° F. Bake 1 hour. Turn off oven; let cake remain in closed oven for 1 hour. Cool away from drafts 2 to 3 hours. Chill at least 8 hours before serving. To cut, use wet, hot, sharp knife.

For a firmer cheese cake, do not separate eggs and add one at a time, beating well after each.   SERVES 10 TO 12

CHAMPION CHEDDAR CHEESE CAKE

Zwieback Crust

1½ cups Zwieback crumbs (about 1 box)	1 tsp. lemon rind
3 Tbs. sugar	6 Tbs. (¾ stick) butter, melted

Roll Zwieback between 2 towels with rolling pin to make crumbs. In a small bowl, mix Zwieback crumbs with sugar and grated lemon rind. Blend in melted butter. Press crust evenly over bottom and sides of a buttered 9-inch spring-form pan. Chill crust while making filling.

Cheddar Cheese Filling

4 packages (8-oz. each) cream cheese	1 cup finely grated mild Cheddar cheese
1¾ cups sugar	½ cup heavy cream, whipped
5 eggs	½ tsp. vanilla
	1 tsp. grated lemon rind

Preheat oven to 500° F.

Beat cream cheese in large bowl. Beat in sugar until creamy. If cheese seems stiff beat in 2 of the eggs so that the cream mixture will be more pliable. Then add remaining eggs. Beat in finely grated Cheddar cheese and beat until yellow specks are almost gone (about 25 minutes). Fold in whipped cream, vanilla, and lemon rind. Pour into crust. Bake 12 minutes; lower heat to 250° F. and continue baking 2 hours, or until firm on top. Cool cake completely on a wire rack. Loosen cake around edge with a knife; release spring and carefully lift off sides. Leave cake on metal base. You may cover with fruit topping. Canned cherry pie filling makes a delicious topping.

SERVES 10 TO 12

LEMON CHEESE CAKE PIE

3 packages (3-oz. each)
    cream cheese
         OR
1 package (8-oz.) cream
    cheese
2 Tbs. butter
½ cup sugar

1 egg
2 Tbs. flour
⅔ cup milk
¼ cup lemon juice
2 Tbs. lemon peel
Graham cracker crumbs

Preheat oven to 350° F.

Prepare 9-inch Graham Cracker pie shell (p. 79).

Cream together cheese and butter; add sugar and egg. Mix well. Add flour, then milk. Stir in lemon juice and peel. Pour into prepared pie shell. Sprinkle with crumbs. Bake 35 minutes. Chill. Good topped with sour cream.

Pies and Pastries

LA PÂTISSERIE

THE ORIENT is responsible for the ancient art of pastry. They used flour and honey to make their dough. As civilization moved forward, pastry making traveled with it. When the Romans defeated the Greeks, among the captured slaves was a master chef, who was put to work in the kitchens of the Caesars. The Caesars, master strategists that they were, ordered their armies to carry the knowledge of the wondrous Greek pastry to the far lands across the Alps.

In the peasant kitchens of medieval France, the flour-and-honey paste was improved upon. Eggs and butter were added and the paste was put into the fire. Out of it came golden clouds, so round, like the shape of a cabbage, they called it "*pâte à choux*." (Cabbage paste).

In 1270, at the time of Philip II of France, honey had been the only sweetening agent used in cooking. About this time sugar was brought into France in abundance from India and China by travelers after the Crusades. Cocoa, a brand-new taste, also came to France from these same places and added a new dimension to the pastry chef's art.

Louis XIV, in 1643, began the glory of French *pâtisserie*. Louis' chef, François Pierre de la Varenne, spread his culinary light in a cookbook. Varenne learned to cook in the kitchens of Henry IV, grandfather of Louis XIV. Henry's wife, Marie de Medici, brought her Florentine chefs to France and from them Varenne got his early training. He published a second book on French pastry. In it were recipes for cake waffles, *gaufres*, and Darioles, a custard. In a raised cake dough recipe, Varenne spoke of the cook who might wish to bake only small quantities in small ovens—the first thought for the housewife who might like to bake.

In the seventeenth century, French pastry cooks roamed the streets of Paris selling their *galettes*, a baked morsel. However, in the eighteenth century an outlaw named Cartouche, disguising his gang as chefs, robbed and murdered people on the streets, and the reputation of the baking profession was at a very low ebb. As a result, pastry cooks became scarce.

It took the French Revolution of 1789 to give the pastry chef a future. Among these newly free men rose Antoine Careme, the most celebrated of all French chefs. He was called the cook of kings and the King of Cooks. He apprenticed with the celebrated Bailly, who was *pâtissier* to Talleyrand. Next he was chief cook to the Prince Regent of England. He then went to St. Petersburg as chef to Czar Alexander and finally was chef to Baron de Rothschild.

His brilliant and delicate creations of sugar and his spec-
tacular desserts were monuments to his artistry. He perfected such classics as *mille-feuille, sultanes, croquem-
bouche,* et cetera. Careme said, "The arts are five in number, painting, sculpture, poetry, music, and architecture,
whose principal branch is *la pâtisserie.*"

T. Hall, who in 1710 contributed to *Queen's Royal
Cookery,* was an Englishman and an acknowledged master
of pies. The English were so fond of them that a whole
section of Cheapside Market, called Pye Corner, was devoted to selling them. At his stall in this market, Hall sold
fried pies that were the granddaddies of our apple turn-
overs.

When, along with our ancestors from Europe, *pâtisserie*
crossed the ocean to the shores of America, it created a new
form called the "pie." The little word PIE is the subject of
much controversy. Some say it is derived from the Latin
pinsere meaning "to beat together." Some say it is an
abbreviation of the French *pâtisserie.*

Pie has changed from a heavy, thick concoction to a
light, airy, melting confection. The American Indian and
the climate has had a profound effect on the development
of this dessert in this country. The Indians cultivated the
tremendous varieties of berries, fruits, and vegetables found
on these shores which have contributed to the myriad fillings for what we think of as the "American Dessert."

Chiffon pies are the elegant ladies of the pastry world.
Chiffon to a woman means a glamorous sweep of gossamer
material; so the chiffon pie is an airy concoction that fairly
floats into the mouth of the discriminating diner. The
chiffon pie is a dream of the American chef, the American
housewife, and the gelatine manufacturers. It is generally
based on gelatine, egg whites, whipped cream, and custards
in various combinations. Special touches are added by a bit

of cordial, a tot of rum, or a spot of extract. Many nations got into the chiffon act. Egypt gave us dates and figs, the Near East gave us ginger, and the ever-important chocolate came from South America. All the fruits get together to do their bit. So the strawberry, raspberry, peach, cherry, apricot, banana, coconut—all make their contribution. Now there are enough varieties of chiffon pies to have one every night of the year, and even one for leap year.

 ## Pie Crusts

STANDARD PASTRY SHELL

1½ cups sifted flour	½ cup shortening
½ tsp. salt	3 Tbs. water, iced

Preheat oven to 450° F.

Place flour and salt in mixing bowl. Cut in the shortening with pastry blender, two knives, or fork. When the consistency of cornmeal, add water a little at a time. On floured board, roll dough into a circle about one inch larger than a 9-inch pie plate. Line and trim off the extra pastry. Fill, or bake unfilled. To bake unfilled, prick all over with fork. Bake 10 to 12 minutes.

QUICK-AS-A-JIFFY CRUST

1⅓ cups sifted flour	⅓ cup vegetable oil
1 tsp. salt	3 Tbs. cold milk

Preheat oven to 450° F.

Mix together flour and salt. Put oil and milk into one cup, but don't stir. Pour all at once into the flour. Stir until mixed. Press with hands into smooth ball. Flatten slightly. Place between 2 sheets of wax paper (12 inches square).

Roll out gently until circle reaches edges of paper. Wax paper will not slip during rolling if the table top is slightly damp. Peel off top paper. If dough tears, mend without moistening by pressing the edges together. Lift paper and pastry by top corners; they will cling together. Place paper side up in 9-inch pie pan. Carefully peel off the paper. Gently ease and fit pastry into pan. Build up fluted edge. Fill or bake unfilled. To bake unfilled, prick all over with fork. Bake for 10 to 12 minutes.

MERINGUE NUT SHELL

2 egg whites	½ cup sugar
⅛ tsp. salt	½ cup chopped nuts
⅛ tsp. cream of tartar	½ tsp. vanilla

Preheat oven to 300° F.

Lightly grease 8-inch pie plate.

Combine egg whites, salt, and cream of tartar in mixing bowl and beat until foamy. Add sugar, 2 tablespoons at a time, beating after each addition until sugar is blended. Continue beating until mixture stands in very stiff peak. Fold in nuts and vanilla. Spoon into prepared pie plate, making a nestlike shell, building sides up ½ inch above the edge of the pan. Bake for 50 to 55 minutes. Cool to room temperature.

GRAHAM CRACKER CRUST

1½ cups fine graham cracker crumbs	¼ cup sugar
	¼ cup melted butter

Add sugar to the graham cracker crumbs. Add melted butter and mix well with fork. Press crumbs into bottom and sides of a 9- or 10-inch plate or 9- or 10-inch spring form.

CREAM CHEESE PASTRY

½ cup butter
1 package (3-oz.) cream cheese

1 cup sifted flour
⅛ tsp. salt

Preheat oven to 450° F.

Cream butter and cheese until smooth. Add half the flour and all the salt to cheese mixture. Blend. Add rest of flour and mix thoroughly. Chill and roll. Fit into 8-, 9-, or 10-inch pie plate. Bake for about 12 minutes. Makes excellent tart shells as well as pie crust.

COOKIE PASTRY CRUST

1 cup sifted flour
½ cup butter
Grated peel of ½ lemon
⅛ tsp. salt

2 Tbs. sugar
1 egg yolk, slightly beaten
Ice water

Preheat oven to 400° F.

Combine first 4 ingredients. Blend in sugar. Add egg yolk and just enough water to make the dough stick together. Shape into ball and chill for 1 hour. Roll on floured board. Fit into 9-inch pie plate. Bake about 15 to 20 minutes.

TOASTED COCONUT CRUST

2 cups moist toasted coconut (one 7-oz. package)
¼ cup butter

Combine coconut and butter. Press evenly over sides and bottom of an oiled 8- or 9-inch pie pan. Chill until firm, about 1 hour. Crust may be frozen.

PIE RECIPES

CHOCOLATE BROWNIE PIE

2 squares unsweetened
    chocolate
2 Tbs. butter
3 large eggs
½ cup sugar

¾ cup dark corn syrup
¾ cup pecan halves
9-inch pie crust
Ice cream or whipped
    cream for topping

Preheat oven to 375° F.

Melt chocolate and butter over hot water. Beat eggs, sugar, chocolate mixture, and syrup with rotary beater. Fold in pecans. Pour into unbaked pie shell. Bake 40 to 50 minutes. Serve slightly warm topped with ice cream or whipped cream. SERVES 6 TO 8

FRENCH GLACÉ STRAWBERRY PIE

1 qt. fresh strawberries
1 package (3-oz.) cream
    cheese
1 baked 9-inch pie shell
    (cooled)

1 cup sugar
3 Tbs. cornstarch
Whipped cream for garnish

Wash, drain, and hull berries. Soften cream cheese by mashing and stirring until smooth. Spread over bottom of pie shell. Cover with ½ of the best berries. Mash and strain the remaining berries until the juice is extracted. If necessary, add water to make 1½ cups of juice. Bring to a boil, and gradually add mixture of sugar and cornstarch. Bring to a boil over low heat, stirring constantly. Boil 1 minute. Cool. Pour over berries in pie shell. Chill about 2 hours. Just before serving, decorate with whipped cream. SERVES 6 TO 8

RASPBERRY CHIFFON PIE

1½ envelopes unflavored gelatine	1 cup raspberry purée,*
	4 egg whites
¼ cup cold water	¼ cup sugar
4 egg yolks	⅛ tsp. salt
1 Tb. lemon juice	¾ cup heavy cream, whipped
½ cup sugar	10-inch baked pie shell

Soften gelatine in water. Combine egg yolks, lemon juice, and ½ cup of the sugar in a small pan. Heat slowly, stirring constantly, until mixture thickens slightly. It should coat spoon. Add gelatine mixture and stir until it dissolves. Stir in the purée and cool until mixture begins to thicken. Beat egg whites with salt until foamy. Gradually beat in rest of sugar until stiff and shiny. Fold into gelatine mixture with ½ of whipped cream. Pour into pie shell and chill for 3 hours. Decorate with rest of whipped cream.

SERVES 6 TO 8

CHOC-FULL-OF-APPLES PIE

5 to 7 tart cooking apples	⅓ cup sugar
9-inch unbaked pastry shell	1 cup prepared biscuit mix
⅓ cup sugar	¼ cup butter
1 tsp. cinnamon	
1 package (6-oz.) semisweet chocolate bits	

Preheat oven to 400° F.

Slice apples thin after peeling and coring them. Arrange half the apples in unbaked pastry shell. Mix the cinnamon with half the sugar and sprinkle half of it over the apples. Then sprinkle on ½ cup of chocolate bits. Repeat with the remaining apples and sugar and cinnamon mixture, but do not sprinkle with chocolate. Mix the remaining ⅓ cup

---

* Purée of raspberries is made by mashing 10 ounces of frozen raspberries or 1½ pints of fresh raspberries and putting through a sieve.

sugar with biscuit mix and cut in butter until it is crumbly. Spread over top of pie. Bake about 40 minutes. Spread the remaining chocolate pieces over top of pie and bake 5 minutes longer. SERVES 6 TO 8

DEEP DISH BLUEBERRY PIE

4 cups blueberries	2 Tbs. lemon juice
2 Tbs. flour	2 Tbs. butter
1 cup sugar	Pastry for 1-crust pie
⅛ tsp. salt	1 qt. vanilla ice cream
¼ tsp. cinnamon	

Preheat oven to 425° F.

Place blueberries in buttered baking dish 10″ × 6½″ × 2″. Blend flour, sugar, salt, cinnamon, and lemon juice and sprinkle over the berries. Dot with butter. Roll dough to ¼-inch-thick crust in the rectangular shape of the baking dish. Arrange crust on top of berry mixture. Bake for 40 minutes. Cut in squares and serve warm, topped with ice cream. SERVES 6 TO 8

PRIZE PRUNE PIE

2¾ cups pitted prunes	1 Tb. lemon juice
Unbaked 9-inch pie shell	½ cup prune liquid
1 egg	½ cup flour
⅓ cup granulated sugar	2 Tbs. sugar
⅛ tsp. salt	2 Tbs. butter

Preheat oven to 425° F.

Cook pitted prunes in water to cover until soft (or cook prunes and pit them). Arrange prunes in pie shell. Beat egg with sugar, salt, lemon juice, and prune liquid. Pour over prunes. Combine flour, 2 tablespoons sugar, and butter. Sprinkle over prunes. Bake for 40 minutes.

SERVES 6 TO 8

ORANGE APPLE PIE

4 or 5 tart apples
3 navel oranges
½ cup sugar
¼ cup flour
¾ cup brown sugar
½ tsp. nutmeg
½ tsp. cinnamon

¼ tsp. allspice
Grated peel 1 orange
Grated peel 1 lemon
Pastry for 2-crust 10-inch
   pie
3 Tbs. butter

Preheat oven to 425° F.

Pare and core apples and slice. Peel oranges, removing all white membranes; slice thin, crosswise. Combine granulated sugar, flour, brown sugar, spices, and peels. Line 10-inch pie plate with pastry. Arrange layers of apples and orange slices in pie shell. Sprinkle with sugar mixture. Dot with butter and put lattice pastry on top. Bake for 15 minutes. Reduce heat to 400° F. and bake 30 minutes longer.   SERVES 6 TO 8

PRALINE PUMPKIN CUSTARD PIE

⅓ cup finely chopped pecans
⅓ cup brown sugar, packed
3 Tbs. soft butter
   9-inch unbaked pie shell
3 slightly beaten eggs
½ cup granulated sugar
½ cup brown sugar, packed
2 Tbs. flour

¾ tsp. salt
¾ tsp. cinnamon
½ tsp. ginger
¼ tsp. cloves
¼ tsp. mace
1½ cups cooked pumpkin
1½ cups light cream, warmed

Preheat oven to 450° F.

Combine first three ingredients and press gently into bottom of pie shell. Prick slightly with fork. Bake 10 minutes.

Combine next 9 ingredients. Add pumpkin and mix well. Gradually add warm cream; mix well. Turn into partially baked pie shell which has been allowed to cool at least 2 minutes. Reduce oven heat to 350° F. and bake 50 to 60 minutes until a metal knife comes out clean when inserted into center of filling.   SERVES 8

CHOCOLATE MOUSSE PIE

1 package (6-oz.) semi-
   sweet chocolate bits
1 egg (whole)
2 egg yolks
1 tsp. rum

2 egg whites
1½ cups heavy cream
   Baked 9-inch pie shell
½ square unsweetened
   chocolate

Melt chocolate pieces over hot water. Remove; beat in egg and yolks, one at a time. Add rum. Beat whites till they form peaks when beater is raised; whip cream. Fold whites and ⅔ of whipped cream carefully into the chocolate mixture. Spoon into shell. Chill. Top with remaining ⅓ of whipped cream. Shave unsweetened chocolate over top of pie.   SERVES 6 TO 8

DRIED APRICOT PIE

2 cups dried apricots
1 cup orange juice
1 Tb. cornstarch
½ cup light brown sugar

   Pinch of salt
2 unbaked 8-inch pie crusts
¼ cup toasted coconut
2 Tbs. butter

Preheat oven to 400° F.

Soak apricots in orange juice for 2 hours. Drain and reserve ⅔ cup of the liquid. Blend cornstarch into the liquid and add brown sugar and salt. Cook mixture, stirring constantly until it thickens. Put apricots in pie shell and pour orange mixture over them. Sprinkle with toasted coconut and dot with butter. Make lattice strips with the remaining pastry dough and arrange on top of pie. Bake for 12 minutes. Reduce heat to 325° F. and bake for 15 minutes more or until pastry is golden brown.   SERVES 6 TO 8

FLUFFY APPRICOT PIE

2 cups dried apricots	2 Tbs. lemon juice
1½ cups cold water	⅛ tsp. salt
2 Tbs. gelatine	3 egg whites
2 tsps. cold water	½ cup sugar
3 egg yolks	¼ cup heavy cream, whipped
¼ cup sugar	8-inch baked pie shell

Soak apricots in water 1 hour. Cook in same water, covered, for 10 minutes. Press apricots through sieve with juice or in a blender; purée should measure 1 cup. Add gelatine to cold water; set aside. In top of double boiler, beat egg yolks. Stir in ¼ cup sugar, lemon juice, salt, and apricots. Cook over boiling water, stirring for about 5 minutes until mixture thickens. Add gelatine, stir until dissolved. Cool. Beat egg whites until stiff, gradually adding remaining sugar. Fold into apricot mixture. Then fold in whipped cream. Pour into shell and chill in refrigerator.   SERVES 6 TO 8

TICKLE-TOP TOASTED COCONUT PIE

1 envelope unflavored gelatine	1 cup hot milk
	1 tsp. vanilla
⅓ cup cold milk	1½ cups whipped cream
3 eggs, separated	9-inch baked pie shell
⅔ cup sugar	1 cup coconut, toasted

Dissolve gelatine in cold milk. Beat egg yolks and sugar with whisk. Add hot milk, beating all the time. Place in top of double boiler and cook until spoon is coated. Remove and add gelatine mixture and vanilla. When it starts to thicken, fold in stiffly beaten egg whites and whipped cream. Put into pie shell. Refrigerate for 3 hours. Remove pie from the refrigerator and sprinkle toasted coconut over the top before serving.   SERVES 6 TO 8

NEW ORLEANS YAMBILEE PRIZE PIE

1 cup mashed sweet potatoes, cooked or canned
⅓ cup brown sugar
¾ tsp. cinnamon
¾ tsp. ginger
Dash of salt

¾ cup scalded milk
2 eggs, well beaten
1 unbaked 9-inch pie shell
Topping
1 cup heavy cream, whipped

Preheat oven to 375° F.

Combine sweet potatoes, brown sugar, cinnamon, ginger, salt, hot milk, and eggs. If fresh sweet potatoes are used, add ½ cup granulated sugar. If canned, pour off liquid. Cool and fill pie shell. Bake for 20 minutes. Sprinkle with topping. Continue to bake for 25 minutes. Serve with whipped cream when cool.

Topping

¼ cup softened butter
½ cup brown sugar

¾ cup pecans, finely chopped

Combine ingredients.   SERVES 6 TO 8

SUMMER NIGHT BERRY CREAM PIE

1 qt. blueberries
1 cup water
1 cup sugar
1 Tb. cornstarch

½ cup water
½ pt. heavy cream
1 tsp. vanilla
1 baked 9-inch pie shell

Simmer 1 pint of blueberries with 1 cup water and sugar. Mix ½ cup water and cornstarch and add to berries. Cook until thick, stirring constantly. Cool. Add the uncooked berries. Whip the cream and add the vanilla. Put into cooled pie shell. Carefully spoon the fruit mixture on top of the whipped cream. It is important that all mixtures be completely cooled before assembling. Refrigerate the assembled pie overnight.   SERVES 6 TO 8

STRAWBERRY RHUBARB PIE

1 lb. fresh rhubarb
¾ cup sugar
½ cup water
2 envelopes unflavored
   gelatine
⅓ cup water

1 package (10-oz.) frozen
   sliced strawberries
⅔ cup evaporated milk,
   chilled
1 Tb. lemon juice
9-inch baked pie shell

Wash rhubarb and cut into 2-inch pieces. Mix sugar and ½ cup water in saucepan. Add rhubarb and bring to a boil. Lower heat and cook until of sauce consistency, about 12 minutes. Sprinkle gelatine over ⅓ cup of water and soften. Add to hot rhubarb and stir until gelatine is dissolved. Add frozen berries and stir until thawed. Cool. Chill until it begins to set. Beat chilled evaporated milk until it will hold a peak. Beat in lemon juice. Fold rhubarb and strawberry mixture into whipped milk lightly but thoroughly. Chill until mixture is slightly firm, about 5 minutes. Put into shell. Chill 2 to 3 hours.   SERVES 6 TO 8

PARTY PRUNE TARTS

2 cups large dried prunes
3 lemon slices
¾ cup prune liquid
¾ cup sherry
1 Tb. cornstarch

1 Tb. water
6 or 8 baked pastry tarts
   (p. 92)
½ cup heavy cream, whipped
   (optional)

Cook prunes with lemon, in water to cover, until soft. Drain, reserving liquid. Pit prunes. Boil liquid down to ¾ cup. Add sherry and pour over prunes and lemon slices. Chill for about 4 hours. Drain off the sherried prune liquid. Stir cornstarch mixed with water into prune liquid. Boil until thick and clear. Add pitted prunes and lemon slices. Chill. Fill shells with prune mixture. Top with whipped cream if desired.   SERVES 6 TO 8

SHERRY CHIFFON PIE

1 envelope unflavored gelatin
⅓ cup cold water
4 eggs, separated
½ cup sugar
⅔ cup sherry

½ cup sugar
½ tsp. salt
9-inch baked pastry shell
½ pt. heavy cream, whipped

Soak gelatine in cold water for 5 minutes. Beat egg yolks with ½ cup sugar until light, and add wine. Cook in double boiler, stirring constantly, until the consistency of custard. Stir in gelatine and cool. Beat egg whites stiff and gradually add ½ cup sugar and the salt. Fold into custard. Pour into shell. Chill about 3 hours. Cover with whipped cream.

SERVES 6 TO 8

TARTS AND PASTRIES

ASSORTED TEA TARTS

Preheat oven to 375° F.

Roll out sweet Tart Pastry (p. 92) ⅛ inch thick. Cut out 12 small rounds and line small tart pans. Set on baking sheet and bake for 10 minutes. Cool and fill with fresh fruits, such as berries, bananas, or cherries. Glaze with melted currant jelly, apricot jam, or other jam or jelly. You can also fill them with fruit preserves to make jam tarts.

SERVES 12

PUFF PASTE

Puff pastry, *pâte feuilleté*, is the most difficult of pastries. Don't be discouraged until you have given it a few tries. In some parts of the country puff-paste sheets are available and they require shaping only. There also is the short method, using the following recipe which makes 12 puff pastry patty shells or 1 large one.

1 lb. sweet butter	½ tsp. salt
1 cup ice water	1½ cups ice water
4 cups (1 lb.) enriched flour, unsifted	

Put butter in a bowl containing 1 cup ice water and knead until it is consistency of putty and free from lumps. Form into ball and extract all pockets of water. Wrap washed butter in wax paper and chill. It must be firm but not hard when used.

On a table top, preferably marble if you have one, sift flour and salt on it in a mound. Work 1½ cups ice water gradually into flour, adding a little more if necessary to make a very firm dough. Work quickly and lightly since this dough should not be handled or kneaded much. Form into a rough ball and chill 30 minutes. Put dough on a floured board and roll it out away from you in a long rectangle ½ inch thick. Turn dough so it is horizontally in front of you. Press butter into a flat cake about ½ inch thick and place in center of dough. Fold the flap of dough on the left to cover the butter, then fold the flap of dough on the right over the left flap. The butter is completely covered with two layers of dough. When folding flaps over, do this lightly to allow for air between layers. Do not press one entire piece down onto the other. Chill for 20 minutes.

Put chilled dough on floured board with the long sides parallel to sides of board and roll it out into a rectangle about ½ inch thick and 20 inches long. Roll only to within ½ inch of either end. Be careful not to let the enclosed butter break through or the air between the layers will be lost and the dough won't puff.

When dough is rolled out into a rectangle, turn it so it is horizontal and fold as before: left-hand third of dough over the center; right-hand third of dough over the two layers, making three layers of dough.

Rolling, turning, and folding like this is called a "turn." Make another turn and chill dough for 20 minutes. Make two more turns, always making sure you have placed dough on table in the same position as before chilling. Two more turns will complete the paste.

If using immediately, make these turns, chill again, then roll, cut and bake. If to be frozen or used a few days later, make the first four turns and store the dough in a bowl, covered with a cloth wrung in cold water, in refrigerator. Save the last two turns until dough is to be used. Chill dough for 20 minutes before rerolling and cutting. Chill dough again before baking.

In France, the term "pastry" (*pâtisserie*) covers all sweet cakes, tarts, petits four, and *gâteaux*. In America, pastry usually refers to pie or tarts while other baked sweets are called cakes, cookies, et cetera. Pastry dough uncooked is pretty much the same in English and French. Here it is puff paste. In France it is *pâte*, not to be confused with *pâté* (which is meat or fish paste.) All doughs are *pâtes* but puff paste is *feiulletage*.

FRENCH PIE PASTRY

5 Tbs. butter	½ tsp. salt
5 Tbs. vegetable shortening	6 or 7 Tbs. cold water
2 cups flour	

Cut butter and shortening into sifted flour and salt with either fingers or pastry blender. Add water until it makes firm dough. Chill for 2 hours before using. Makes enough for one pie.

NORMANDY PEACH TART

Tart Pastry

2 cups sifted flour	4 egg yolks
4 Tbs. sugar	½ cup of soft butter

Make a mound of the flour. Put the sugar, egg yolks, and butter into a well in the center of the mound. With your fingers, work the ingredients into a paste. Shape it into a round ball. Knead lightly, put it into wax paper and chill 1 hour. Roll out, fit into 9-inch pie plate or tart pans.

Peach Filling

6 ripe peaches	2 eggs
¼ cup butter	¼ cup sugar
¼ cup sugar	1½ cups milk
Tart Crust (above)	3 Tbs. kirschwasser
2 Tbs. flour	

Preheat oven to 375° F.

Dip peaches in boiling water and let stand for 1 minute. Then slip skins from the peaches. Cut into thick slices. Sauté in butter and ¼ cup sugar over high heat until sugar caramelizes. Arrange peaches in pastry shell or shells. Mix flour with eggs and remaining sugar. Stir in milk and kirschwasser. Pour over the peaches in the shell. Bake for 30 minutes, or until custard sets.

QUICK PUFF PASTE

1 lb. sweet butter	¼ tsp. salt
4 cups flour	1½ cups ice water

Knead butter until it is the consistency of soft dough and free of lumps. Wrap and chill in refrigerator.

Sift flour onto tabletop in a mound. Sprinkle flour with salt. Gradually work ice water into flour, enough to make it very firm. Work quickly, rubbing the flour and water together until dough cleans the table. Do not knead the dough, but form it lightly into a ball and chill for 30 minutes. Put dough on floured board and roll into rectangle ½ inch thick. Turn butter into center of dough and fold dough to cover the butter. Press the folded edges firmly together and chill for 20 minutes. Place dough on floured board into long rectangle about ½ inch thick. Roll lightly, being careful not to let the butter break through. Turn dough and fold as before, right side to center and left side over the right, making three layers. Chill for 20 minutes. Do this twice more and let chill for 20 minutes each time before rolling it out and baking.

NAPOLEONS

Preheat oven to 450° F.

Roll out puff paste into rectangle ⅛ inch thick and cut into 3 strips 2½ inches wide by about 16 inches long. Place strips on baking sheet lined with brown paper. Prick the surface of the dough with a fork and chill. Then bake strips for 10 minutes. Reduce temperature to 350° F. and continue baking for another 10 minutes. Cool strips and put together with Pastry Cream (below) or whipped cream, sweetened and flavored to taste. Dust top with confectioner's sugar and cut strips crosswise with a serrated knife into squares or oblongs.

Pastry Cream

1½ cups milk	¼ cup flour
½ cup sugar	½ tsp. vanilla
4 egg yolks	

Scald milk. Mix together sugar and egg yolks, beating until creamy. Add flour, mixing to blend. Add scalded milk gradually, stirring until well combined. Cook until cream almost boils, stirring constantly. Add vanilla. Cool, stirring occasionally to prevent a film from forming.

CHOCOLATE ANGEL PIE IN MERINGUE SHELL

4 squares sweet chocolate	1 cup heavy cream
3 Tbs. black coffee	Meringue Nut Shell
1 tsp. vanilla	(p. 79)

In a saucepan over low heat, combine sweet chocolate with coffee, stirring until chocolate is melted and mixture is smooth. Cool and stir in vanilla extract. Whip heavy cream. Fold into melted chocolate and turn filling into meringue shell. Chill pie for 2 hours.   SERVES 6 TO 8

STRETCHED STRUDEL DOUGH

2 cups flour	⅔ cup warm water
¼ tsp. salt	(approximately)
White of 1 egg	⅓ cup melted shortening

Working quickly, sift flour and salt. Add egg white, mix a little, then add sufficient water to make a soft dough. Knead well on a board until no longer sticky, tossing and stretching dough to make it elastic. Brush with shortening and cover with warm bowl for about one hour. Place on well-floured tablecloth on a large table and roll a little. Brush again with melted shortening and with hands under the dough, palms down, pull and stretch dough gently from the center. Then, using finger tips, palms up, pull gradually around the edges until sheet is as thin as tissue and as large as the table. To complete, follow directions under fillings.

ROLLED STRUDEL DOUGH

1 egg	2 cups flour
¼ cup melted shortening	¼ teaspoon salt
6 Tbs. warm water	½ teaspoon baking powder

Beat egg, add shortening and water and then the flour mixed with salt and baking powder. Knead lightly until dough is very soft, a little oily but not sticky. Cover and set in warm place for one hour. Place on floured tablecloth and roll as thin as possible. Finish by stretching and pulling gently until thin as tissue paper. A small piece can be rolled thin more successfully than larger one. Divide dough in halves and fill each part separately.

INSTANT STRUDEL DOUGH

Open 1 can of refrigerator crescent rolls (8 rolls to a can) and knead into a ball the dough for all 8 rolls. Then roll out as thin as you can get it, pulling and stretching it a bit to help get it thin. Add any of the suggested fillings and proceed as you would for homemade strudel or follow recipe for French Pastry or Cream Strudel (p. 96).

PREPARED STRUDEL DOUGH SHEETS

Strudel sheets or leaves can be purchased in special stores and markets. They are kept refrigerated or frozen until ready for use. Leave at room temperature for 3 hours sealed in the cellophane package before using.

CHEESE STRUDEL

Strudel dough	Grated rind of 1 lemon
1 lb. pot cheese or farmer cheese	2 egg yolks
	½ cup sugar
½ cup raisins	2 eggs whites, beaten stiff

Preheat oven to 400° F.

Make same dough preparations as for Apple Strudel.

Put cheese through the ricer, add raisins and lemon rind, and add egg yolks beaten foamy with sugar. Fold beaten egg whites into mixture. Follow the procedure for Apple Strudel, substituting cheese mixture for apple mixture. Bake for 25 to 30 minutes.   MAKES 12 TO 15 SLICES

APPLE STRUDEL

Strudel dough
½ stick (¼ cup) of butter, melted
4 to 5 medium green apples peel and cut in small cubes
¼ cup chopped pecans or walnuts
½ cup sugar
½ cup raisins
½ tsp. cinnamon
Grated rind of 1 lemon

Preheat oven to 400° F.

Put on damp cloth strudel dough rolled very thin or stretched paper thin. Paint lightly with melted butter, using pastry brush. Mix together apples, nuts, sugar, raisins, cinnamon, and lemon rind. Place mixture on edge of dough sheets nearest to you, in one long strip. Roll like a jelly roll by taking the edge of cloth near you and let it roll over. Place strudel on buttered pan and brush top with butter. Mark individual portions with sharp knife. Bake 25 to 30 minutes until golden brown.   MAKES 12 TO 15 SLICES

CHERRY STRUDEL

2 cups pitted cherries (fresh or canned)
½ cup dry bread crumbs

Follow Apple Strudel recipe, substituting cherries for apples. Sprinkle with bread crumbs before rolling up.

MAKES 12 TO 15 SLICES

FRENCH PASTRY OR CREAM STRUDEL

Preheat oven to 375° F.

Use 4 sheets of strudel dough.

Place one sheet of strudel dough upon another, spreading each one with melted butter and sprinkling lightly with sugar and corn-flake crumbs. (Dough may be cut in half to fit pan, making 4 layers). Bake for 5 to 10 minutes. Cut while hot into 3-inch strips and put aside. When ready to serve place fillings between baked strips and cut into serving pieces. Fill with Chocolate Filling or any of the following:

Whipped cream sweetened and flavored with vanilla, whipped cream and berries, or

flavored custard with tart jelly.

Chocolate Filling

½ pt. heavy cream   ½ cup confectioner's sugar
3 Tbs. bitter cocoa

Blend and chill for 3 hours. Whip until stiff and place between baked pastry layers. SERVES 10 TO 12

DRY FRUIT STRUDEL

Strudel dough   ½ tsp. cinnamon
¾ lb. dried apricots   1 cup white raisins
1 grated lemon   1 cup coconut
1 grated orange   1 cup corn-flake crumbs
¾ cup sugar   1 Tb. melted butter
1 cup walnuts, chopped

Preheat oven to 400° F.

Cover apricots with boiling water and soak overnight. Drain off water and chop fine. Grate entire lemon and orange on grater, including pulp. Add half to apricots with sugar; blend. Combine remaining lemon and orange with walnuts, cinnamon, raisins, coconut, and corn-flake crumbs. After strudel dough has been stretched thin, spread walnut-fruit mixture evenly over entire sheet. Drip melted butter over all. Spread all-fruit mixture in thin line across one end of sheet, about 4 inches from the edge. Fold edge over fruit and roll up dough, lifting tablecloth up to raise and roll dough. Place roll in well-greased pan and let stand 15 minutes. With sharp knife slice part way through at 1-inch intervals. Bake 1 hour.

BAKLAVA

A famous Greek speciality so easy to make with the prepared phyllo found in Greek speciality shops.

1 lb. phyllo sheets	2 cups honey
1 lb. cut-up walnuts or	3 cups water
almonds	3 cups sugar
1 lb. butter	Dash of cinnamon

Preheat oven to 250° F.

Melt butter. Butter bottom of 12 × 16-inch baking dish. Working quickly with the phyllo because the sheets dry out, spread one sheet on bottom of pan and trim to fit. Brush sheet with melted butter. Repeat sheets and butter three or more times. Cover generously with nuts. Top with a sheet of phyllo; butter it. Repeat with sheet and buttering. Cover with layer of nuts. Continue in this fashion until all the nuts have been used. Then continue spreading the phyllo and buttering each sheet until all the phyllo has been used.

Using a sharp knife with a sawing stroke, cut the sheets into about 50 diamond-shaped pieces. Sprinkle a few drops of water on top. Bake for 2 hours.

Make syrup by combining honey, water, sugar, and cinnamon and boiling it for ½ hour. When baklava is baked, pour COOL syrup on HOT baklava. Allow to stand at least 24 hours before serving.   YIELD: ABOUT 50 PIECES

SCHAUM TORTE

8 egg whites	½ cup granulated sugar
1½ cups granulated sugar	2 cups strawberries
1 tsp. vinegar	1 pt. whipped cream
1 tsp. vanilla	

Preheat oven to 250° F.

Beat egg whites until stiff; add 1½ cups sugar gradually, two tablespoonfuls at a time. Beat in vinegar and vanilla and gently fold in remaining sugar to make a meringue.

Line two baking sheets with wax paper and on each trace two 8-inch circles. Fill one circle with a layer of meringue ¼ inch thick. On the other circle make a ring about 1 inch high and 1½ inches wide. Bake meringues for 30 to 40 minutes or until crisp but not at all colored.

Remove from wax paper to a cake rack to cool and dry.

When ready to serve place solid circle on plate and put the ring on top. Fill the shell thus formed with 2 cups of strawberries, sliced, sweetened, and folded into a pint of whipped cream.

9

Refrigerator Desserts

VENEZUELAN ESPONJOSO

This dessert caused an uproar in Washington's diplomatic circles—all the way up to the White House. Three incorrect versions of the recipe circulated until *McCall's* magazine produced the right one. It was conceived by a cook at the Venezuelan Embassy who needed some strong persuasion to give away her secrets.

12 egg whites	Boiling water
2 boxes (1 lb. each) super- fine sugar	English Sauce

In a large bowl of electric mixer let egg whites warm to

room temperature for about 1 hour. Meanwhile, place 1½ cups sugar in medium-size heavy skillet. Caramelize by cooking over high heat, stirring until sugar is completely melted and begins to boil. Resulting syrup should be medium brown. Pour hot syrup quickly into 3-quart Pyrex casserole; turn and rotate casserole until bottom and sides are thoroughly coated. Be careful. It will be HOT! Set on wire rack and let cool.

Beat egg whites until very stiff—about 8 minutes. Gradually beat in 1 pound of sugar, taking about 3 minutes. Scrape sides of bowl with rubber scraper. Continue beating 15 more minutes. Meanwhile (about 5 minutes before beating time is up) place ¾ cup sugar in heavy medium skillet and caramelize as directed above. Remove from heat; let stand 20 to 30 seconds to thicken a bit. With beater at medium speed gradually pour this syrup into beaten egg whites; scrape sides of bowl with rubber scraper. Return to high speed and beat 12 more minutes.

Turn mixture into prepared casserole, spreading evenly. Set in large shallow pan; pour boiling water around casserole to 1-inch depth. Bake 1 hour at 250° F. or until meringue rises about 1 inch above top of casserole and seems firm when gently shaken. Remove casserole from water; place on wire rack to cool. Refrigerate at least 6 hours or overnight. Or freeze.

To unmold: Run a small spatula around edge of meringue to loosen. Hold casserole in pan of very hot water at least 1 minute. Invert on serving dish and serve with some of English Sauce (page 35) poured over meringue; the rest passed in a pitcher. SERVES 16

MOCHA POCA SORTA TORTA

3 egg whites
1 cup superfine sugar
1 tsp. vanilla extract
25 unsalted crackers, finely
   rolled
1 cup finely chopped pecans

1 Tb. instant coffee powder
1 pt. heavy cream
2 Tbs. confectioner's sugar
2 Tbs. cocoa
   Whipped cream and chocolate curls for garnish

Preheat oven to 350° F.

Beat egg whites until foamy; gradually beat in superfine sugar, 2 tablespoons at a time, beating well after each addition. Add vanilla; beat until soft peaks form. Combine cracker crumbs, pecans, and coffee. Gently fold into meringue mixture. Spoon into a lightly greased and floured 9-inch pie plate. Pull up mixture with back of spoon to form peaks around edge of plate. Spread center evenly. Bake for 30 minutes. Cool thoroughly on wire rack. Will keep a day or two, well covered. Whip cream until stiff; fold in confectioner's sugar and cocoa; mound in center of shell. Decorate with more whipped cream, chocolate curls.

SERVES 6

PASHKA
✈ *Russian Easter Dessert*

4 packages (3 oz. each)
   cream cheese
½ cup sweet butter, softened
2 tsps. vanilla extract
½ tsp. fresh lemon juice
¾ cup sugar
½ cup sour cream
1 cup chopped, blanched
   almonds

1 cup diced mixed glacé
   fruit
1 cup seedless raisins
6-in. diameter new clay
   flower pot
½ cup whipped cream
   Additional glacé fruit
   (optional)

Beat together until fluffy the cream cheese, butter, and vanilla. Stir in lemon juice, sugar, sour cream, almonds, glacé fruit, and raisins. Line a clean clay pot with 3 layers of cheesecloth and pour mixture into it. Place pot on a tray and chill 6 hours or overnight. Just before serving turn out onto a tray. Remove cheesecloth. Decorate as desired with whipped cream and fresh or glacé fruit. SERVES 12

GRAPE BAVARIAN

1 package (3-oz.) lemon-flavored gelatine
1 cup boiling water
1 cup bottled grape juice

1 cup heavy cream, whipped
Additional whipped cream
   (optional)

Dissolve gelatine in boiling water. Add grape juice. Chill until slightly thickened. Blend in whipped cream. Spoon into 1-quart mold. Chill until firm. Garnish with additional whipped cream if desired. SERVES 6 TO 8

STRAWBERRY BAVARIAN

1 qt. hulled fresh strawberries
2 envelopes unflavored
   gelatine
¼ cup cold water
½ cup sugar

3 Tbs. cherry-flavored liqueur
2 cups heavy cream, whipped
Whole fresh strawberries
   for garnish

Purée the strawberries in sieve or blender. Strain if puréed in blender. Soften gelatine in cold water and add to purée with sugar. Heat and stir until gelatine is dissolved. Cool and add cherry-flavored liqueur. Chill, stirring occasionally until thickened. Fold in whipped cream. Place in mold or serving bowl and chill until set. If placed in mold, unmold to serve. Top with whole fresh strawberries.

BLOSSIE'S SPECIAL

½ lb. vanilla wafers, crushed
¾ cup butter
1 lb. confectioner's sugar
1 can (4-oz.) crushed pineapple, drained

2 eggs, room temperature
6 Tbs. cognac
1 pt. heavy cream, whipped

Butter an 8 × 8-inch pan; cover with half of wafer crumbs. Cream the butter and sugar; stir in ⅔ of the pineapple; add the eggs and mix well. Add the cognac and stir well. Pour half the mixture over the crumbs in the pan. Layer on remaining crumbs and filling. Top with the whipped cream mixed with remaining crushed pineapple, dropped from a spoon. Cover and refrigerate at least overnight. It will keep four to five days.   SERVES 8

FRESH COCONUT MOUSSE

1 qt. milk
1½ cups sugar
¼ tsp. salt
1 tsp. almond extract
2 cups grated fresh coconut
4 Tbs. unflavored gelatine
5 egg whites

1 pt. heavy cream
Additional freshly grated coconut for garnish
Green leaves for garnish (optional)
Caramel Sauce (p. 32)

Oil 2 melon molds (or molds of your choice. You may also use just one mold.)

Bring milk to boil, reduce heat and add sugar, salt, and extract. Add coconut and the gelatine which has been softened in a little cold water. Allow to stand until slightly thickened. Beat egg whites until stiff. Whip cream. Fold them into coconut mixture. Pour into prepared molds. When ready to serve, turn out onto and decorate platter with freshly grated coconut and green leaves. Serve with Caramel Sauce (page 32).   SERVES 10 TO 12

BOURBON ON A CLOUD

6 Tbs. sugar	3 egg whites
1 envelope unflavored gelatine	6 Tbs. sugar
3 egg yolks	1 cup heavy cream
½ cup bourbon	Ladyfingers

In top of double boiler, blend half the sugar with gelatine. Add beaten yolks; blend. Trickle in bourbon. (Too speedy addition of bourbon tends to "cook" eggs; blend thoroughly as you add slowly.) Place over simmering, not boiling water and cook, stirring constantly, until mixture thickens slightly and coats metal spoon (about 10 minutes). Beat egg whites until foamy. Continue beating while adding remaining sugar. Beat until stiff, shiny peaks form. Gradually fold in yolk mixture. Let stand in refrigerator until cool, about 20 minutes. Beat cream until soft peaks form. Fold into pudding mixture. Pour half into 1½-qt. mold lined with ladyfingers. Layer ladyfingers and remaining mixture. Chill six hours or overnight.   SERVES 8

LEMON CUSTARD FLUFF

3 eggs, beaten	2 doz. ladyfingers
1 cup sugar	Whipped cream for topping
Juice of 1½ lemons	1 cup toasted coconut
1 cup heavy cream	

Line an 8-in.-square baking dish with ladyfingers.

Cook eggs, sugar, and lemon juice in top of double boiler until thick. Cool. Whip cream and add to custard. Pour half the custard mixture over ladyfingers. Put on another layer of ladyfingers. Cover with remaining custard. Set in refrigerator overnight. Top with whipped cream and toasted coconut. Cut in squares and serve.   SERVES 8

DOUBLE CHOCOLATE AFFAIR

Chocolate Cups

8 oz. semisweet chocolate   1 Tb. butter
8 foil or paper muffin cups

Melt chocolate over hot water. Add butter and stir with dry wooden spoon until smooth. Coat the inside of the foil muffin cups with a thin layer of chocolate, carefully coating the sides as well as the bottom. Refrigerate or freeze to harden. When completely hardened peel off the foil and fill cups with either the following filling or ice cream. Shells can be made in any type of foil pans, either ring or cake-pan varieties. The same method is followed.

Semisweet Chocolate Mousse Filling

5 eggs, separated   5 Tbs. cold water
3 Tbs. brandy or rum   1 pt. heavy cream, whipped
8 oz. semisweet chocolate

Beat egg yolks with brandy or rum until light but not frothy. Set aside. Melt chocolate and water over hot water. Cool slightly and beat in egg yolks. Beat whites until stiff but not dry and stir part of them into chocolate mixture. Fold in remaining whites very gently. Then fold in whipped cream and fill the chocolate cups with mixture. Chill well in refrigerator or freeze in freezer after covering with foil.

SERVES 6

COLD LEMON SOUFFLÉ

24 ladyfingers   1 cup granulated sugar
 2 envelopes unflavored   Pinch of salt
    gelatine   4 Tbs. grated lemon rind
½ cup lemon juice   2 cups heavy cream, whipped
10 eggs   Apricot Marmalade Sauce

Cut piece of wax paper long enough to circle a 3-qt.

soufflé dish. Fold in half lengthwise and in half again; butter one side; wrap around the outside of the dish so that paper is 2 inches above rim. Line dish with ladyfingers, cutting to fit bottom of dish. Soften gelatine in lemon juice and dissolve over hot water. Place eggs, sugar, and salt in double boiler over simmering water. Beat about 10 minutes, until eggs are thick and light in color, and fill a 3-qt. saucepan ¾ full. Add gelatine and lemon rind and beat a few more seconds. Cool a bit, fold in whipped cream and pour into prepared soufflé dish. Chill several hours at least, preferably overnight. Remove wax paper and serve with Apricot Marmalade Sauce (see p. 33). Serves 12

CHOCOLATE TORTE SUPREME

½ cup strong cold coffee
1½ Tbs. sugar
2 Tbs. Grand Marnier
1 cup sweet butter
2 large eggs

12 oz. semisweet chocolate, melted
1 package vanilla wafers
1 cup heavy cream, whipped
1 to 2 Tbs. Grand Marnier

Line a bread pan with aluminum foil, allowing enough over in the edges to cover the top.

Combine cold coffee with sugar and 2 tablespoons Grand Marnier. Cream butter. Beat in eggs and melted chocolate. Arrange a layer of vanilla wafers on the bottom of the lined pan. Sprinkle generously with coffee liquid, then spread with chocolate cream until all is used up. Top with a layer of wafers. Fold foil over top and set an identical pan on top of the cake. Weight down with heavy stones or brick. Let ripen in refrigerator at least 12 to 16 hours, preferably overnight. To serve, carefully fold back top foil. Turn torte out on serving platter. Frost top and sides with whipped cream lightly flavored with Grand Marnier. Slice thin.

Serves 8 to 10

TO THE QUEEN'S TASTE ICEBOX CAKE

16 ladyfingers
8 oz. sweet cooking chocolate
3 Tbs. sugar
Dash of salt
3 Tbs. water

6 eggs, separated
1 tsp. vanilla
⅓ cup brandy (optional)
½ pt. whipped cream for
garnish

Line 9-in. spring-form pan with ladyfinger halves. Melt chocolate, sugar, salt, and water in top of double boiler. Cool. Add egg yolks to cooled chocolate mixture, one at a time, beating well after each addition. Add vanilla and brandy. Mix well. Beat egg whites until stiff. Fold into chocolate mixture. Pour into spring form. Chill at least 3 hours or until firm. Remove spring form sides and top with whipped cream.   SERVES 8

STRAWBERRY REFRIGERATOR SOUFFLÉ

4 tsps. unflavored gelatine
¼ cup cold water
1 package (16-oz.) quick-
frozen strawberries,
thawed

4 eggs, separated
2 Tbs. lemon juice
⅛ tsp. salt
½ cup sugar
1 cup heavy cream

Sprinkle gelatine over cold water. Let stand to soften. Drain strawberries, measuring juice. Pour ¾ cup of juice into top of double boiler. Beat egg yolks slightly; stir into juice. Add gelatine. Place over simmering water. Stir until gelatine dissolves. Remove from heat. Stir in lemon juice and salt. Chill until consistency of unbeaten egg whites.

Press strawberries through a fine sieve. Stir into gelatine mixture until blended. Beat egg whites until foamy; add sugar and beat until mixture holds stiff peaks. Beat gelatine mixture with rotary beater until smooth. Fold in egg whites. Whip cream and fold into gelatine mixture. Make a collar by cutting a piece of wax paper long enough to circle a 1½-quart soufflé dish. Fold in half lengthwise and in half again; butter one side; wrap around outside of dish so paper is 2 inches above rim. Pour in soufflé mixture. Chill until set—at least four hours. Remove collar before serving.

SERVES 10 TO 12

ISLAND DREAM ICEBOX CAKE

16 ladyfingers
1 package of raspberry
   gelatine
1 cup hot water
12 marshmallows, regular size

2 cups fresh or frozen raspberries
½ cup almonds, chopped
1½ cups heavy cream,
   whipped
3 slices pineapple

Line a 9-in. spring form with ladyfingers. Dissolve gelatine in hot water and add marshmallows while the gelatine mixture is still hot. When gelatine begins to set, fold in raspberries, almonds, and whipped cream. Put the pineapple slices in bottom of a 9-inch spring mold and pour mixture over the pineapple. Chill 12 hours.

SERVES 8

BLENDER CHOCOLATE BAVARIAN CREAM

¼ cup of cold water or milk
¼ cup hot strong coffee
1 envelope unflavored
   gelatine
1 package (6-oz.) semi-
   sweet chocolate pieces

1 Tbs. sugar
2 egg yolks
1 heaping cup crushed ice
1 cup heavy cream
1 package (16) ladyfingers

Line a 9-inch spring mold or other type mold with ladyfingers.

Put water or milk, coffee, and gelatine into blender. Cover and blend on high speed for 40 seconds. Add chocolate, sugar, and blend for 10 seconds. Add yolks, ice, and cream. Blend 20 seconds. Pour mixture into prepared mold. Chill until set.

SERVES 8

CHOCOLATE BOMBE SUPREME

1 large angel food cake mix
  (10-oz.)
1 cup semisweet chocolate
  pieces
1 package (8-oz.) cream
  cheese
¾ cup bottled maple-
  blended syrup or pure
  maple syrup
½ tsp. instant coffee powder
¼ tsp. salt
1 cup heavy cream
½ cup semisweet chocolate
  pieces
1½ tsps. butter
3 Tbs. coffee-flavored
  liqueur
1 cup heavy cream

Preheat oven to 375° F.

Make the cake mix according to package directions. Pour 6 cups of batter into ungreased 2½-quart ovenproof bowl. (Pour remaining batter into a 1-qt. ovenproof bowl to use as dessert another time.) Bake both cakes 30 minutes. Invert large bowl, resting edges on wire racks or pans to cool. Scoop out center, leaving 1½-inch thick shell. Loosen this shell from bowl.

Melt 1 cup chocolate over hot, not boiling, water. In bowl, with electric mixer at medium speed, beat the cream cheese until light and fluffy. Then slowly beat in syrup, coffee powder, and salt. Fold chocolate into cheese mixture. Beat 1 cup cream until stiff; fold into cheese mixture, then pour into shell. Cover with freezer paper and freeze.

On wax paper draw a rectangle 10″ × 8″; grease a cookie sheet and lay wax paper on it. Over hot, not boiling, water melt ½ cup chocolate pieces with butter; stir. Spread thinly over wax-paper rectangle. Refrigerate until firm; invert and peel off paper. Cut into shapes with miniature cookie or aspic cutters or cut into 1½-inch squares with sharp knife. Cut squares in half, triangles. Refrigerate.

About 2 hours before serving remove bombe from freezer; let stand at room temperature 15 minutes. Then loosen from bowl with spatula and invert on serving plate. Drizzle liqueur over surface. Beat remaining cream until stiff and use to frost bombe. Decorate with chocolate shapes. Refrigerate until serving time.   SERVES 12

CHOCOLATE MOUSSE I

6 oz. semisweet chocolate
4 Tbs. water
4 eggs, separated
¾ cup sugar
¼ cup orange liqueur
   (Grand Marnier)

10 Tbs. soft butter
1 cup heavy cream, whipped
1 Tb. sugar
⅛ tsp. salt

Melt chocolate with water over hot water. Mix egg yolks with ¾ cup of sugar. Heat and stir until mixture thickens. Do not boil. Remove from heat and add liqueur. Beat butter into chocolate mixture and add to egg mixture. Fold in whipped cream. Beat whites until stiff with 1 tablespoon sugar and salt and fold into chocolate mixture. Pour into individual dishes or large bowl and refrigerate until well chilled.   SERVES 8

CHOCOLATE MOUSSE II

½ lb. dark sweet chocolate
6 Tbs. coffee

5 eggs, separated
2 Tbs. rum

Cut up chocolate and dissolve with coffee over low heat. Remove. Quickly stir in beaten egg yolks and rum. Fold in stiffly beaten egg whites. Pour into 8 small pots and refrigerate at least 4 hours.   SERVES 8

MOCHA REFRIGERATOR CAKE

2 doz. ladyfingers, split
3 oz. unsweetened chocolate
½ cup granulated sugar
¼ cup strong coffee
4 eggs, separated

1 cup butter
1 cup confectioner's sugar
1 tsp. vanilla or rum
½ cup heavy cream

Line bottom and sides of straight sides 3" × 5" × 11" loaf pan with ladyfingers.

Melt chocolate over hot water. Combine granulated sugar, coffee, and slightly beaten egg yolks. Add to melted chocolate. Cook until thickened. Cool. Cream butter with ½ cup confectioner's sugar. Add flavoring and combine with chocolate mixture. Beat egg whites stiff and fold in remaining ½ cup confectioner's sugar. Fold the egg whites into cooled chocolate mixture. Spread ⅓ chocolate mixture over ladyfingers; top with layer of ladyfingers. Repeat, making 3 layers of chocolate mixture with ladyfingers between and on top. Chill several hours or overnight. Remove from pan. Garnish with whipped cream.   SERVES 8

LEMONADE PUDDING

2 slightly beaten egg yolks
1½ cups milk
1 package (3 to 3¼ oz.)
    regular vanilla pudding
    mix
1 package (3-oz.) cream
    cheese, softened
1 can (6-oz.) frozen
    lemonade concentrate,
    thawed

2 egg whites
¼ cup sugar
½ cup vanilla wafer crumbs
2 Tbs. chopped walnuts
2 Tbs. butter, melted

Combine egg yolks and milk. Prepare pudding, following package directions, using egg-milk mixture as the liquid. Add cream cheese and beat smooth with electric or rotary beater; stir in lemonade concentrate. Cover surface with wax paper and cool 10 minutes. Beat smooth again. Beat egg whites to soft peaks; gradually add sugar, beating to stiff peaks. Fold egg whites into pudding. Combine crumbs, nuts, and butter. Sprinkle half the crumb mixture into 6 sherbet glasses. Spoon in pudding and top with remaining crumb mixture. Chill. Serves 6

10

Frozen Desserts

FROZEN DESSERTS HAVE A HISTORY

THE FIRST recorded use of any substance resembling ice cream took place in the reign of Nero Claudius Caesar in A.D. 54–68. He demanded that snow be brought from the mountains. Fruit juices and other flavorings were added to the snow, which was brought by swift runners and the result was a dish that resembled modern fruit ices. These messengers were the ancestors of our Good Humor men. It was so difficult to get mountain snow that the dish was fit only for an emperor.

The secret of this concoction was lost with Nero's defeat. It was gone from recorded history until the thirteenth century when Marco Polo returned from Cathay with a recipe for a dish that contained milk in addition to the original ingredients of Nero's snow dish.

Its popularity grew in Italy, spread to France and the court of Henry II (1519–1559), and finally to England to the court of Charles I (1600–1649). Charles tried to keep the formula a secret so that it could be served only at his dinners, but there is always one blabbermouth in the kitchen. In 1675, a Sicilian pastry cook named Procopio went to Paris and opened the first ice-cream parlor. The people went wild over the cold sweetness. Soon there were two hundred ice-cream parlors around Paris.

Ice-cream manufacture was brought to America in the 1600's. The first recorded evidence was in a letter written by William Bladen (1673–1718), Governor of Maryland, stating that this dessert was being made in his territory. By the end of the eighteenth century the first ice-cream parlors began to appear in New York, and George Washington had two freezers installed at Mount Vernon.

Thomas Jefferson learned to make ice cream while in France, writing down the recipe in his own hand. On one occasion he served for dessert at the White House crisp, hot pastry with a center of ice cream. Shades of Baked Alaska. Ice-cream cones, introduced at the Louisiana Purchase Exposition in St. Louis in 1904, were a smashing success.

BLACKBERRY MOUSSE

4 cups blackberries	1 qt. heavy cream
1 cup sugar	Additional berries for
1 tsp. lemon juice	garnish

Crush blackberries with a fork and sprinkle them with sugar. Let them stand for 1 hour. Put the fruit mixture through a sieve to remove the seeds. Stir lemon juice into purée and fold in the whipped cream. Put into 1½-quart mold. Seal the mold and freeze mousse without stirring. Serve garnished with whole berries.   SERVES 6

COCONUT RASPBERRY BOMBE

¼ cup butter
2 Tbs. sugar
2⅔ cups coconut macaroon
   crumbs (14 cookies)
2 pts. softened vanilla ice
   cream

⅓ cup coarsely chopped
   walnuts
1 pt. raspberry sherbet
   Raspberry Melba Sauce

Cream butter until light and fluffy; gradually add sugar; then gradually add crumbs. Press onto bottom and sides of a 7-cup mold, preferably bombe shaped. With back of spoon or spatula spread vanilla ice cream as evenly as possible about 1 inch thick over crumb shell. Press walnuts into bottom and sides of ice cream. Place in freezer to harden ice cream. Spoon raspberry sherbet into center of mold; freeze.

Unmold by dipping into warm water and turn out on chilled plate. Serve with Raspberry Melba Sauce (p. 33) if desired.   SERVES 8 TO 10

CHOCOLATE PECAN TORTE

3 egg whites
⅛ tsp. salt
1½ cups sifted confectioner's
   sugar
1½ cups finely crushed short-
   bread cookie crumbs
1 cup finely chopped pecans

2 squares semisweet
   chocolate, chopped
½ tsp. vanilla
2 qts. peppermint,
   pistachio, or vanilla ice
   cream, softened
Chocolate Sauce (p. 32)

Preheat oven to 350° F.

Beat egg whites and salt until foamy. Gradually add sugar, beating until mixture will hold very stiff peaks. Fold in cookie crumbs, pecans, chopped chocolate, and vanilla. Line a baking sheet with brown paper. Draw two 8-inch

circles on the paper and grease circles with butter. Divide
meringue mixture between the two circles, spreading evenly
so that the edges are the same thickness as the centers. Bake
18 to 20 minutes. Partially cool on rack. While still warm,
carefully loosen edges of meringues with a spatula. Leave
on paper until cold. Remove meringues from paper; place
one on plate. Spread about half of softened ice cream over
it. Top with the second meringue. Spoon remaining ice
cream over top. Freeze until firm. Top with Chocolate
Sauce (p. 32). SERVES 10

TORTONI SQUARES

⅓ cup chopped toasted
    almonds
3 Tbs. melted butter
1 cup fine vanilla wafer
    crumbs

1 tsp. almond extract
3 pts. vanilla ice cream,
    softened
1 (12-oz.) jar apricot or
    peach preserves
    Whipped cream (optional)

Line an 8-inch square pan with aluminum foil.

Combine almonds, butter, crumbs, and extract. Mix well.
Save ¼ cup of crumb mixture for top. Sprinkle half of remaining mixture over bottom of prepared pan. Spoon half
the ice cream over crumb mixture; drizzle with half the
preserves and sprinkle with crumb mixture. Repeat this
process, using remaining ice cream and preserves. Sprinkle
reserved crumbs over top. Store in freezer until ready to
serve. Cut in squares and garnish with whipped cream if
desired. SERVES 9

FROZEN STRAWBERRY SOUFFLÉ

2 packages (10-oz. each)
    frozen sliced strawberries
    (thawed) or 1 qt. fresh
    strawberries
6 eggs, separated
1 cup sugar
½ cup Grand Marnier
1 cup sugar

⅓ cup orange juice
3 cups heavy cream, whipped
    Red food coloring
¼ cup chopped walnuts
    Strawberries for garnish
    Strawberry Sauce (p. 36)
    Whipped cream for garnish

Prepare an 8-cup soufflé dish. Make "collar" to extend 3 inches above the top of the dish, using a double strip of aluminum foil 4 to 5 inches wide and long enough to circle the outside of the dish. Secure the collar with paper clips and a rubber band.

Purée the thawed frozen sliced strawberries or fresh, using a blender. (It will make about 2 cups.) Beat egg yolks until thick and lemon-colored and beat in 1 cup of sugar. Add half the strawberry purée, mixing well. Cook over simmering water, in top of double boiler until mixture thickens, about 15 to 20 minutes. Stir often; cool. Stir in ½ cup Grand Marnier.

In small saucepan combine 1 cup sugar and ⅓ cup orange juice. Heat, stirring until sugar dissolves. Then cook without stirring until a soft ball forms when a little of mixture is dropped into cold water, or to 232° F. on a candy thermometer.

Beat egg whites until very stiff. Very slowly pour hot syrup in a thin stream over them, beating at high speed, until all syrup is used and mixture stands in stiff peaks. Cool. Whip cream. Fold into strawberry-egg yolk mixture along with remaining purée. Fold in meringue. Stir in a few drops of red food coloring. Turn into soufflé dish and freeze until firm.

To serve, remove collar and press chopped walnuts into the sides of the soufflé. Decorate with fluffs of whipped cream and a few fresh strawberries. Return to freezer. Serve with Strawberry Sauce (p. 36). It is also good without sauce.   SERVES 12

PULL-IT-OUT CHOCOLATE SOUFFLÉ

A hot soufflé that can be prepared ahead of time. It must be frozen to work; you can pop soufflé out of the freezer into the oven.

⅔ cup cream
1 package (8-oz.) cream
   cheese
1 package (6-oz.) semisweet
   chocolate bits

6 eggs, separated
½ tsp. cream of tartar
⅓ cup confectioner's sugar

Line a 2-quart soufflé dish with aluminum foil. Blend cream with cream cheese over very low heat. Add chocolate pieces and stir until melted. Remove from heat. Beat yolks until thick and lemon-colored. Gradually blend into cooled chocolate mixture. Beat egg whites until foamy. Add cream of tartar. Gradually add sugar, beating constantly. Beat until stiff. Fold into chocolate mixture. Fill foil-lined soufflé dish to within ½ inch from top. Freeze. Lift soufflé in aluminum foil from soufflé dish, wrap, and return to freezer. It will keep for one month.

To bake, remove foil and replace frozen soufflé in original dish. Bake at 300° F. for 1 hour or until firm to the touch. Serve immediately.   SERVES 6 TO 8

REGENCY TARTS

2 (4½-oz. each) boxes chocolate-covered almond clusters
2 cups miniature marshmallows

½ cup milk
1 cup heavy cream, whipped
8 to 10 tart shells (p. 92)
Additional whipped cream for garnish (optional)

Heat chocolate-covered almond clusters and marshmallows with milk in double boiler, stirring until well blended. Chill until slightly thickened; mix until well blended. Fold in whipped cream. Pour into tart shells; freeze. Serve right from freezer, garnishing with whipped cream if desired.

SERVES 8 TO 10

COFFEE ICE CREAM PIE

Crust

2 Tbs. butter
2 squares (1-oz. each) unsweetened chocolate
2 Tbs. hot milk

⅔ cup sifted confectioner's sugar
1½ cups shredded coconut

Butter 9-inch pie plate.

Melt butter and chocolate over hot water; blend. Stir milk into confectioner's sugar; add to chocolate mixture; mix well; stir in coconut. Press onto bottom and sides of prepared pie plate. Chill in refrigerator.

Filling

1 qt. vanilla ice cream
2 tsps. instant coffee

¼ cup chopped pecans
8 pecan halves

Stir ice cream to soften; mix thoroughly with instant coffee and chopped pecans. Spread in pie shell, swirling the top. Decorate with pecan halves. Freeze until firm. Take out 10 to 15 minutes before serving.

SERVES 8

HAARLEM PUFFS

¾ cup water
6 Tbs. butter

¾ cup flour
3 eggs

Bring water and butter to a boil. Add flour all at once and stir mixture briskly until it leaves sides of pan and forms ball. Transfer to mixer bowl and beat in eggs one at a time, beating well after each addition. Drop in heaping tablespoonsful on buttered baking sheet. Bake at 375 degrees for 35 minutes. Cool and split. Fill.

Filling

1 pt. heavy cream, whipped
½ cup sifted confectioner's
    sugar

2 oz. grated, dark, sweet
    chocolate
3 Tbs. confectioner's sugar

Whip cream stiff; fold in sugar and chocolate. Use to fill puffs. Dust with confectioner's sugar. Freeze. Defrost about 20 minutes before serving. SERVES 8

PRIZE PRUNE PARFAIT

⅔ cup sugar
¼ cup water
6 egg yolks
1 cup prune purée (Use jars
    of junior foods or put
    pitted prunes in
    blender.)

2 Tbs. brandy
2 cups heavy cream

Boil sugar and water for 5 minutes. Beat egg yolks until light and gradually add syrup, beating constantly. Cook over hot water stirring until creamy mixture thickens. Remove from heat and beat until cool. Stir prune purée and brandy into cream mixture. Fold in heavy cream, beaten stiff. Freeze without stirring for 2½ to 3 hours.

SERVES 6 TO 8

LYNN'S LEMONS
Tangy!

6 lemons   1 pt. lemon-custard ice cream

Cut top off lemons and a piece from bottom so that they will stand firmly. Scoop out lemon pulp and plunge the lemon shells into boiling water for 5 minutes. Drain and cool. Fill with lemon-custard ice cream. Cover and store in deep freeze. Can be used as a dessert, and also as a savory with a meat or turkey course.

11

Custards, Puddings, and Soufflés

PAST TRIUMPHS

IN THE early 1700's "sillibubs" arrived on the scene. These foamy light custards of eggs, milk, white wine or sherry and spices were also called "syllabubs" and "sillibubbles," which is the name we like best! Syllabub was a favorite of British Queens and almost every one of them had a recipe for it in a special royal cookbook that has been kept for many generations. Anne Boleyn was the first Queen to give instructions for making "Syllibub under the cow." This was listed in the Royal Cook Book that was started in 1540. Queen Victoria's favorite was made with equal quantities of cream and milk, flavored with orange water and white wine, sweetened with sugar and frothed with egg white. A notation in Victoria's girlish hand says: "If you will have it of a red color, put in clarett instead of white wine."

SYLLABUB

2 cups milk
3 Tbs. sugar
2 eggs, separated
Grated rind of ½ lemon or
orange

1 cup medium dry sherry
Grated nutmeg

Beat milk, sugar, and egg yolks until smooth. Stir in grated rind and wine. Refrigerate. Shortly before serving, beat egg whites to a froth, stir into other ingredients, grate a little nutmeg over top. Serve from punch cups or as custard over cake in sherbet dishes. SERVES 4 TO 6

In 1533, Catherine de Medici, Henry II's Queen of France, brought her Florentine chefs with her to the Court of France. The Italian dishes made in her kitchens were a revelation to the French. The Court was delighted with "iced cream," the winy custard Zabaglione, which the French gallicized to *sabayon*. The little cakes layered with custard and elaborately garnished began a new trend in sweets.

ZABAGLIONE

8 egg yolks
1 cup confectioner's sugar

½ cup Marsala, Madeira, or
cream sherry

Combine egg yolks, sugar, and wine and place in top of double boiler (over hot, not boiling water). Beat constantly with wire whisk or portable electric mixer until it doubles in volume and begins to thicken. Pour at once into 4 sherbet glasses. Serve either chilled or hot. Stiffly beaten egg whites may be folded into the custard after it is removed from hot water. Zabaglione may be served as sauce over cake, puddings, or Baba au Rhum; if to be used as sauce, divide above ingredients in half. SERVES 4

INDIAN PUDDING

1 cup yellow cornmeal	⅛ lb. butter, softened
¼ cup sugar	1½ tsps. cinnamon
¼ tsp. salt	1 tsp. ground ginger
¼ tsp. baking soda	¾ tsp. ground cloves
2 eggs, beaten	6 cups hot milk
½ cup dark molasses	Vanilla ice cream

Preheat oven to 425° F.

Mix together all the ingredients but the milk and ice cream. Beat well. Add 3 cups hot milk. Mix well and pour into a buttered 2-quart baking dish or casserole that you can bring to the table. Bake until mixture comes to boil. Reduce heat to 225° F. Stir thoroughly into casserole three cups hot milk and bake for five hours. Let pudding stand for 30 minutes or until set. Serve warm with scoops of vanilla ice cream. SERVES 12

BAKED CUSTARD

3 eggs	3 cups milk, scalded
½ cup sugar	1 tsp. vanilla
¼ tsp. salt	Nutmeg

Preheat oven to 325° F.

Beat eggs. Stir in sugar and salt. Add milk and vanilla. Pour into 6 buttered custard cups. Sprinkle with nutmeg. Set in shallow pan in boiling water 1 inch deep. Bake one hour. Test by inserting silver knife in the center. If it comes out clean, the custard is firm and done. SERVES 6

RIZ À L'IMPERATRICE

½ cup rice	2 Tbs. cold water
1¼ cups milk	3 Tbs. apricot preserves
4 egg yolks	⅓ cup chopped citron
½ cup sugar	⅓ cup chopped candied
¾ cup hot milk	lemon peel
1-inch piece vanilla bean	⅓ cup chopped candied
or 1 tsp. vanilla extract	orange peel
1 envelope unflavored	½ cup kirsch
gelatine	1½ cups heavy cream

Overnight, marinate citron, candied orange, and lemon peel in kirsch.

Wash the rice in cold water; cover it well with cold water in saucepan and bring to boil. Simmer for 2 minutes; drain in a sieve and rinse with cold water. Return rice to pan and cook it with 1¼ cups milk until very tender. Do not stir while cooking.

In the top of a double boiler combine the egg yolks, sugar, remaining hot milk, vanilla. Cook over boiling water, stirring until sauce is smooth and thick. Soften gelatine in cold water; stir into mixture. Strain the custard through a fine sieve. Add the rice and apricot preserves and blend thoroughly. Cool.

Whip the cream until stiff and blend with marinated fruits. Then add to cooled rice pudding. Pour into a 2-quart mold and chill overnight. Unmold on platter.

SERVES 8

EASY PUDDING SOUFFLÉ

1 package chocolate	3 eggs, separated
pudding mix	1 tsp. vanilla
1½ cups milk	

Preheat oven to 350° F.

Prepare chocolate pudding in saucepan by adding milk to packaged mixture and following package directions. Beat egg yolks until thick and light. Beat egg whites until they form soft peaks. Stir hot pudding into beaten yolks; then gently fold in beaten egg whites and vanilla. Turn mixture into 1½-quart buttered casserole. Bake in pan of hot water for about 45 minutes until puffed.   SERVES 4

GRAND MARNIER SOUFFLÉ

8 to 10 ladyfingers	5 egg yolks
2 Tbs. Grand Marnier liqueur	5 Tbs. sugar
2 Tbs. butter	6 egg whites
1 Tb. flour	1 tsp. vanilla
½ cup hot milk	

Preheat oven to 375° F.

Moisten ladyfingers lightly with Grand Marnier. Melt butter in saucepan, blend in flour and cook slowly until mixture begins to turn golden. Stir in hot milk and vanilla and cook slowly for 5 minutes, stirring constantly with wire whip. Beat egg yolks until light with 4 tablespoons sugar and add to sauce. Beat egg whites until stiff; add remaining sugar during the last minutes of beating. Fold stiffly beaten egg whites very carefully into mixture. Cut into mixture with slotted spoon. Pour half of mixture into a buttered 6-cup soufflé dish. Cover with split ladyfingers and fill the dish with rest of mixture. Bake for 18 to 20 minutes or until puffed and lightly brown.   SERVES 6

CHRISTMAS PLUM PUDDING

2 cups finely chopped beef
 suet
5 oz. white raisins
5 oz. dark raisins
5 oz. currants
3 oz. chopped lemon peel
2 oz. chopped blanched
 almonds
¾ cup dry bread crumbs
¾ cup flour

1 tsp. pumpkin-pie spice
3 eggs, beaten
1 cup brown sugar
½ tsp. salt
Juice and rind of 1 lemon
6 oz. ale
6 oz. beer
3 oz. rum
3 oz. brandy

Mix all ingredients together well moistening with ale, beer, rum, and brandy. Fill a buttered bowl or container ¾ full and tie a cloth (heavy muslin) over the top of the bowl. Put the bowl on a rack in a large pot of boiling water. The water should be deep enough to reach halfway to the top of the bowl. Simmer for 3 hours. Cool before storing.

When ready to serve reheat the pudding in a kettle of water for about 1 hour. Remove cloth from top; turn pudding out on a plate by inverting bowl. Sprinkle pudding with sugar. Pour warm rum or brandy over the top and light up. Serve flaming. Often hard sauce is served with it (p. 33).   SERVES 8 TO 10

POMPADOUR PUDDING

1 cup flour
2 tsps. baking powder
½ tsp. salt
¾ cup granulated sugar
2 Tbs. cocoa
½ cup milk
1 tsp. vanilla

2 Tbs. shortening, melted
¾ to 1 cup chopped walnuts
 (optional)
1 cup brown sugar
¼ cup cocoa
1¾ cup hot water

Preheat oven to 350° F.

Grease 8-in. square or round cake pan or pudding dish.

Sift together flour, baking powder, salt, granulated sugar, and 2 tablespoons cocoa. Add milk, vanilla, and shortening; mix until smooth. Add nuts. Pour into prepared cake pan, or pudding dish.

Mix brown sugar and ¼ cup cocoa. Sprinkle mixture over the batter. Pour hot water over entire batter. Bake for 40 to 45 minutes. This makes a pudding-like cake with a rich chocolate sauce that goes to the bottom of the pan.

If desired, top with marshmallows, return to oven to melt. Delicious also topped with vanilla-flavored whipped cream.   SERVES 4 TO 6

RICE PUDDING

½ cup seedless raisins
2 Tbs. rum
1 tsp. lemon juice
Grated rind of 1 lemon
¼ cup uncooked rice
2 cups milk

¼ tsp. salt
2 Tbs. butter
2 eggs, separated
⅓ cup sugar
Dash of nutmeg

Soak raisins in rum, lemon juice, and rind for an hour. Cook rice, milk, and salt in top of double boiler over boiling water until rice is tender (1 hour). Stir butter into hot rice. Beat egg yolks lightly. Pour rice mixture into yolks; cool. Add raisins and liquids in which they were soaked.

Preheat oven to 325° F.

Beat egg whites until stiff, adding sugar gradually. Fold into rice mixture very carefully. Pour into greased 1-quart casserole and sprinkle with nutmeg. Set in pan of hot water and bake 30 minutes. Serve cold.   SERVES 4 TO 6

RICE CREAM

4 eggs, beaten
1 cup sugar
⅛ tsp. salt
1 qt. milk, scalded

1 tsp. vanilla
2 Tbs. raisins
2 cups cooked rice

Preheat oven to 350° F.

Combine eggs, sugar, and salt. Stir in scalded milk and vanilla. Add raisins and cooked rice. Pour into a 2-quart baking dish. Set dish in pan of hot water. Bake for 45 to 50 minutes. Stir once or twice while cooking. Serve hot or cold.   SERVES 8

BEST CHOCOLATE SOUFFLÉ

2 Tbs. butter
4 Tbs. flour
1 cup milk
4 Tbs. water

6 Tbs. sugar
2 oz. unsweetened chocolate
4 egg yolks
4 egg whites

Preheat oven to 325° F.

Melt butter, add flour. Add milk and cook until smooth. Add the water and sugar to the chocolate, heat and when chocolate is shiny, mix it with cream sauce; cool. Stir in the egg yolks, beaten light and fluffy. Fold in stiffly beaten egg whites very gently. Bake in greased 9-inch soufflé dish or pudding dish with straight sides. Put in pan of hot water to bake. Bake for 30 to 40 minutes. Test with knife. If knife is clean when thrust in middle, soufflé is done.

SERVES 4 TO 5

ORANGE SOUFFLÉ

3 Tbs. butter
3 Tbs. flour
¾ cup milk
½ cup sugar
Dash of salt

¼ cup fresh orange juice
1 Tb. grated orange rind
4 eggs, separated

Preheat oven to 350° F.

Melt butter; add flour and blend. Slowly add milk, stirring constantly. Cook and stir until thickened. Add sugar, salt, orange juice and rind. Blend and cook 3 to 4 minutes. Remove from heat, cool slightly. Add well-beaten egg yolks to mixture. Fold in stiffly beaten egg whites. Pour into an unbuttered 1½-quart soufflé dish. Bake in pan of hot water for 45 to 50 minutes. Five minutes before baking is completed (after about 40 min.), sprinkle granulated sugar over soufflé. Put back in oven for 5 minutes.

SERVES 4 TO 5

WILLA MAE'S BREAD PUDDING

3 cups of pieces of bread
   (ends and crusts are
   acceptable)
2 cups milk
1 egg
1 tsp. baking powder
   (heaping)

½ cup sugar
½ cup raisins
7 Tbs. butter, melted
1 Tb. flour

Preheat oven to 400° F.

Combine bread and milk well. Add egg, baking powder, sugar, raisins, melted butter, and vanilla. Mix. Bake in a 9-inch square baking pan for 40 to 45 minutes. Best served warm, but good any way.

SERVES 6 TO 8

12

Fruit for Dessert

FRUIT—ITS HONORABLE PAST

FRUIT IS a delightful ending to a delicious, filling meal. In Europe much ceremony is made of the serving of the dessert fruit. It is brought to the table with bowls of water so that you may wash the fruit as you eat. In America, melons and berries are served in their fresh splendor as are many other types of fruits.

Ever since the first shipment of bananas was sent from Cuba to New York in 1804 Americans have been addicted to the banana. Captain Lorenzo Baker sailed out of Boston in 1870, and his destination was Jamaica. He found nothing to load his boat with but bananas. He brought the exotic fruits back to America where they were readily received.

They were the big food sensation at the 1876 Philadelphia Centennial Exposition.

Melons were first found in southern Asia. Travelers to that part of the world ate them and carried away seeds. The early Greeks and Romans were lovers of the melon. Tiberius thought so highly of melon that he ordered them to be served daily throughout the year.

Apples have had the best press agent in the world—Eve. Nothing more need be said.

PERFECTLY EASY PRUNE WHIP
This takes 15 minutes

1½ cups sieved, cooked prune (or prepared junior food prunes)
½ tsp. grated lemon rind

1 Tb. lemon juice
Dash of nutmeg
2 egg whites
¼ cup sugar

Combine prunes, lemon rind and juice, and nutmeg. Beat egg whites until foamy; beat in sugar gradually. Continue beating until mixture stands in stiff, glossy peaks. Fold egg-white mixture into prune mixture. Chill well. Serve with either poured or whipped cream.   SERVES 4 TO 5

BAKED APPLE CRISP

3 cups sliced apples
½ cup flour
1 cup brown sugar

¼ cup butter
⅓ cup walnuts

Preheat oven to 375° F.

Arrange apple slices in square 6″ × 10″ pan. Combine flour and sugar. Cut in butter until pieces are size of large peas. Add nuts. Sprinkle over apples. Bake for 40 to 45 minutes, or until tender. Serve hot with whipped cream or nippy cheese.   SERVES 4

NEW ORLEANS BANANAS FLAMBÉ

2 Tbs. butter
4 tsps. brown sugar
2 bananas
Pinch of cinnamon

1 tsp. banana liqueur
1 oz. rum or brandy
Vanilla ice cream

Mix butter and brown sugar in saucepan. Cook over medium heat until caramelized. Cut bananas in quarters. Add and cook until tender. Add cinnamon and liqueur; stir. Add heated rum or brandy to top of mixture. DO NOT STIR. Light. Spoon over vanilla ice cream while flaming.

SERVES 2 TO 3

SEEDLESS GRAPES WITH SOUR CREAM

½ pt. sour cream
2 Tbs. brown sugar

1 lb. seedless grapes,
thoroughly chilled

Place a mound of sour cream, sprinkled with sugar, on a dessert plate. Make a well in the center and put into it about 15 grapes. Dip grapes in sugared cream and pop into your mouth.

SERVES 4

COCONUT BAKED BANANAS

1⅓ cups brown sugar
½ cup coconut cream (see
below)
1 Tb. rum
1 tsp. vanilla

¼ tsp. salt
8 bananas, peeled, quartered
1 cup heavy cream, whipped
and sweetened

Combine sugar and coconut cream. Cook until lightly brown (about 5 minutes). Don't caramelize too much. Add rum, vanilla, and salt. Put bananas in dish and pour sauce over them. Chill. Serve with whipped cream.

Coconut Cream
Preheat oven to 400 degrees.

Punch two holes in coconut with ice pick and drain off milk. Bake coconut 15 minutes. Tap coconut shell until it falls off. Pare off dark outer skin. Cut meat into ½-inch cubes. Put 1 cup coconut milk (add water if necessary to make 1 cup) and 1 cup meat in blender 30 to 40 seconds. Drain through sieve. SERVES 4

BLENDER APPLESAUCE
Unusual

4 apples
¼ cup water or fruit juice

¼ cup sugar
⅛ tsp. cinnamon

Wash apples and cut in quarters. Remove cores and cut in eighths. Soak in cold salt water for 10 min. Put ¼ cup of water or juice and 4 apple wedges in blender. Blend at high speed. Add remaining wedges, sugar, and cinnamon and blend again. If cooked sauce is desired, eliminate cold water bath and heat apples, water, sugar, and cinnamon to a boil and then blend. SERVES 2

BANANA FRITTER BAHAMA

4 bananas
2 cups prepared biscuit mix
¼ cup flaked coconut

½ cup milk
1 egg
2 tsps. confectioner's sugar

Peel, halve, and then quarter bananas. Mix biscuit mix, coconut, milk, and egg until well blended, though the batter should be lumpy. Coat bananas completely with batter and fry in hot fat until golden brown on both sides. Drain on absorbent paper. Dust with confectioner's sugar when ready to serve. SERVES 4

ORANGE SNOW

1 envelope unflavored gelatine	2 Tbs. lime juice
½ cup cold water	¾ cup fresh orange juice
¼ cup sugar	2 egg whites
¼ tsp. salt	2 oranges, sectioned

Sprinkle gelatine on cold water in top of double boiler to soften. Place over boiling water and stir until gelatine dissolves. Add sugar, salt, lime juice, and orange juice. Stir until sugar is dissolved. To chill quickly half fill lower part of double boiler with ice cubes and water. Set upper half of double boiler over ice water. Chill until slightly thickened. Beat with rotary beater until mixture holds shape. Fold in stiffly beaten egg whites. Fold in orange sections. Chill until firm in 9- or 10-inch mold.　　　　SERVES 4

BLUSHING BROILED GRAPEFRUIT

3 grapefruit	6 maraschino cherries
6 Tbs. sugar, brown sugar, honey, maple syrup	Sherry (1 tsp.) per half or maraschino cherry juice (optional)
Cinnamon or nutmeg	
2 Tbs. butter	

Prepare grapefruit halves by removing seeds and cutting around sections. Sprinkle each with a tablespoon sugar and dash of cinnamon or nutmeg. Dot each with 1 teaspoon butter. Broil slowly for 15 minutes or until slightly brown on top. Top with cherry.　　　　SERVES 6

TRUE BLUEBERRY PUDDING

1 qt. fresh blueberries	4 slices firm white bread
½ tsp. cinnamon	½ cup butter
2 Tbs. sugar	⅔ cup sugar
1 cup heavy cream, whipped	

Wash and drain blueberries. Mix cinnamon and 2 table-spoons sugar. Whip cream until stiff. Fold cinnamon and sugar mixture into whipped cream and chill. Dice bread into squares after removing crusts. Sauté bread cubes in butter until golden brown and coat thoroughly with ⅔ cup sugar. Just before serving reheat cubes, add berries, and warm them well. Serve with a dollop of the chilled whipped cream mixture.   SERVES 4

FRENCH GRAPES AND CANTALOUPE IN SOUR CREAM

2 cups seedless grapes	3 Tbs. sugar
1 cup cantaloupe balls	1 tsp. grated fresh orange peel
1 cup sour cream	Small cluster seedless grapes

Cut grapes in half and mix with cantaloupe, sour cream, sugar, and orange peel. Toss lightly and chill. Serve in sherbet glasses. Garnish with clusters of grapes.

SERVES 6

HARVEST MOON FRUIT COMPOTE

1 package (1 lb.) dried prunes	1 can (1 lb. 5-oz.) cherry pie mix filling
½ package (11-oz.) dried apricots	2 cups water
1 can (13½-oz.) pineapple chunks, undrained	¼ cup sherry

Preheat oven to 350° F.

In 9″ × 9″ × 2″, or 2-quart round baking dish, layer prunes, apricots, and pineapple. Combine remaining ingredients and pour over fruit. Cover and bake for 1½ hours. Serve hot. It is also delicious to refrigerate and serve thoroughly chilled.   SERVES 8

BAKED AMBROSIA

1 can (1 lb.) apricot halves	½ cup orange juice
1 can (1 lb.) peaches	¼ cup brown sugar
1 can (1 lb.) purple plums	½ tsp. shredded lemon peel
3 or 4 thin orange slices, halved	2 Tbs. butter, melted
	½ cup flaked coconut

Preheat oven to 425° F.

Drain canned fruits thoroughly. Arrange with unpeeled orange slices in a shallow baking dish, 9″ × 9″ × 2″. Mix orange juice and sugar; pour over fruit. Drizzle melted butter over. Sprinkle coconut over all. Bake for 15 minutes. Serve warm. SERVES 8

FESTIVAL OF FRUITS
The perfect summer dessert

½ lb. seedless green grapes	4 sliced fresh peaches
½ pt. sour cream	1 pt. strawberries
½ cup brown sugar	

Use a glass or crystal bowl or pitcher. The beauty of this simple dessert should be seen. Place a layer of grapes in bowl. Top with sour cream and sprinkle with brown sugar. Repeat with peaches and then strawberries. Chill overnight. The brown sugar mingles with the sour cream and flavors the fruit. SERVES 8 TO 10

13

Cheese as a Dessert

CHEESE IN ANCIENT TIMES

ARCHAEOLOGISTS HAVE established that cheese was well known to the Sumerians in 4000 B.C. Egyptian and Chaldean artifacts also establish its existence.

The Greeks had a deity, Aristaeus, who was considered the giver of cheese. Homer sang of cheese, and in *The Odyssey* he told of Polyphemus who "curdled half the milk and set it aside in wicker baskets." These wicker baskets were called *formos* in Greek, and the word then became *forma* in Latin; the Italian *formaggio* developed and the French made it *fromage*.

Latin also had *caseus* for cheese, the Germans made it *kase*, the Dutch *kaas*, the Irish *cais*, the Welsh *caws* and the Spanish *queso*. In Anglo Saxon it was *cese* which later became *cheese*.

The Greeks gave cheese to their children as a goody (would that we could!). The mainstay of the Olympic athletes' diets was cheese. Wedding cakes of the time were invariably cheese cakes.

Marco Polo brought reports of cheese from his travels in the East.

There were great cheeses that came out of the monasteries of the Middle Ages—the soft ripening cheeses for which France is so famous. Charlemagne, while staying at a monastery, was found picking blue-green bits out of the cheese he had been served for dinner. The monks protested that he was wasting the best part of the Roquefort, so the King tasted it and said it was magnificent. He had two cases of the cheese delivered every year to his palace. In 1411, Charles VI issued a decree restricting the name Roquefort to cheese made in the Roquefort district of the Causses. They were still battling interlopers as recently as the 1960's.

Cheese for Today's Desserts

The custom of serving cheese at the end of the meal is largely European. In Italy and France, where the *pâtisserie* is superb, diners can have the best of two worlds—excellent cheese and fruit followed by the sweet. Cheese harmonizes with many variations of food and will do well as the last course to enhance almost any dinner. There are exceptions: it is not well to serve cheese following a very rich meat such as pork, or poultry such as roast duck. It should be avoided in menus to which it would be alien. For example, cheese doesn't go very well with a Chinese or Japanese dinner, a paella, or a hot Indian curry. Conversely, an Italian or

French meal without some cheese either during or following would be difficult to imagine.

Dinner cheeses are of two varieties. Some are called dessert cheeses and others are called after-dinner cheese. Dessert cheeses are very delicate creamy cheese such as Hablé Crème Chantilly, and the double and triple *crèmes* such as Petit Suisse. After-dinner cheeses include Brie, Camembert, and Stilton. These can be followed by a sweet.

Petit Suisse is a small, very rich cream cheese, unsalted, cylindrical in shape and is delicious sprinkled with fine sugar and eaten with crisp biscuits.

Triple Crème Parfait is an excellent cheese with a burnt-orange crust streaked with white mold, indicating that it has lain on straw during its curing period. It is about 3 inches in diameter and 2¼ inches high.

Brillat-Savarin differs from other triple-*crèmes* mostly in its texture. When cold, it is a little grainy. However, this graininess tends to disappear the longer the cheese sits at room temperature.

Le Roi has wrinkled beige crust with fine lines of white mold and a brilliant yellow paste, which at room temperature is threaded through with what looks like tiny rivulets of melted butter.

Boursault and *Boursin* are superior triple-*crèmes*, and unlike all the others are packaged in paper, not in boxes.

Fondue de Savoie au Raisin—more commonly called Grape Cheese. The rind is covered with the black grape skins and seeds from the local wine pressings. The texture is white and buttery and the flavor mild.

Crème Danica is the only entirely different cheese of major importance to be invented in the past forty years. Its inventor, Henrik Tholstrup, a descendant of three generations of cheesemakers, decided that he would make a cheese with Brie texture but without its faults. This he did in 1957 and the result was Crème Danica. This cheese ripens very evenly and after being at room temperature for a couple of hours, becomes glossy through the entire stick.

Brie—the greatest cheese of all to cheese lovers. Made in the province of Brie and adjoining districts, these are large, round, and very thin. Overripe Brie will be easily detectable. It tastes too strong; it smells too much; it looks too runny. The top crust almost meets the bottom and the cheese spreads out all over the plate. The perfectly ripened Brie has a taste part mushroom, part cream, part cognac, part earth. The texture is like heavy honey. It has the gloss of satin and it should be uniform throughout.

Stilton—an English cheese, the invention of Mrs. Paulet of Wymondham in 1800. Stilton is one of the great cheeses of the world. Made of the richest cow milk, it matures without refrigeration. It is set apart from other blue cheeses by its distinctive flavor which is a blue taste with an undertone of Cheddar.

Roquefort-Thenblue—veined cheese, made entirely of rich ewe's milk. It is the oldest blue-veined cheese of France, its production dating back years. It is made in Aveyron, S.W. France, where it matured in the famous local caves of Roquefort. Creamy but crumbly in texture, its flavor is delicious and somewhat pungent.

Coulommiers—originated in the department of Seine-et-Marne. It is made from rich cow's milk and is round, flat and packed in wood-chip boxes. It ripens as Brie.

Camembert—a well-known soft cheese of Normandy, made from rich cow's milk. It originated from the village of Camembert around 1791. Camembert softens on ripening.

Pont L'Eveque—a square cheese in a wood-chip box. It is named after the small town in Calvados. Somewhat close curd, thin-rinded and full-flavored when mature.

Pipo Crem—an exquisitely delicate blue that comes in

cylindrical shape is higher in cream content than other blue cheeses. Its body is pale yellow because of this. It does not have the sharp bite of Roquefort or Gorgonzola. Lovers of mild cheese will particularly enjoy this because it has much of the quality of double crèmes.

Gorgonzola—first made in the Po Valley in the ninth century and named for a village near Milan. According to the legend these were originally unveined cheeses and were used by the farmers to pay for their wines in the local shops when they had no money. The winekeepers kept them in their cellars where they eventually developed a green mold. Gorgonzola is superlatively rich and creamy.

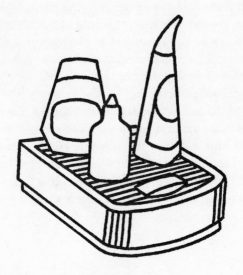

14

Desserts for Dieters

DESSERTS AND DIETS

IN AMERICA one of the chief preoccupations of both men and women is to achieve perfection of the human form. Would that we could find a Shylock who would take a pound of flesh! Instead we must diet, exercise and massage. Compounding the problem is the medical fact that cholesterol and excess weight can shorten your life. But what is a meal without dessert? The answer is the diet dessert.

Most people need not be on a diet constantly, but on occasion, when the weight creeps up, it is easy to limit calories without pain by using a lower-calorie dessert. Also, the family can be served such a dessert without their knowing the difference, or realizing that it is "diet" food!

Some desserts can be reduced in calories by simply deleting sugar from their content or by substituting a low-calorie sweetener. Be creative. Discover by experimenting which can successfully become a diet delight. For example, some soufflés are not spoiled by this method, but a cake will be a fiasco if sugar is omitted.

Food processors have contributed to the general good by discovering and marketing "sugar substitutes." They enable us to ban the sweets without missing them, for the substitutes give sweetness without caloric content. We submit the following quite delicious recipes as our contribution to the body beautiful.

Sugar Substitutes

SWEET 'N' LOW—Concentrated powdered sugar substitute; 1 packet (1 gram) equals sweetness of 2 teaspoons sugar.

SACCHARIN OR SWEETA—Drops of liquid concentrate; 2 drops equal sweetness of 1 teaspoon of sugar.

TWIN—Powdered sugar substitute. Spoon for spoon equals sweetness of sugar.

SUCARYL—Liquid sweetener; ⅛ tsp. or 1 tablet for sweetness equal to 1 teaspoon sugar.

Always read and observe package directions for use.

COFFEE AND CREAM DESSERT

¼ cup evaporated milk, whipped
1 envelope unflavored gelatine
¼ cup cold water
2½ tsps. liquid sugar substitute or concentrated powdered

1 oz. unsweetened chocolate
1 cup skim milk
½ cup cold strong coffee
2 eggs, separated
1 tsp. vanilla

To whip evaporated milk chill in freezer until ice crystals form around edge, then beat with rotary beater until stiff.

Soften gelatine in cold water. Combine sugar substitute, chocolate, milk, and coffee in saucepan. Stir over low heat until chocolate melts. Bring to boiling point. Beat egg yolks. Stir hot mixture into beaten egg yolks. Return mixture to saucepan, cook over low heat for 1 minute, stirring constantly. Remove from heat; add softened gelatine, vanilla. Mix thoroughly, cool. When cold and beginning to set, fold in stiffly beaten egg whites and whipped evaporated milk. Spoon into sherbet dishes. Chill.

56 calories
SERVES 9

COCONUT SURPRISES

3 oz. cream cheese
4 (1 gram) packets concentrated powdered sugar substitute
¼ tsp. grated orange rind

¼ tsp. grated lemon rind
1 tsp. chopped walnuts or pecans
¼ cup shredded coconut, toasted

Work cheese with spoon until light and fluffy. Thoroughly mix in sugar substitute, grated rinds, and nuts. Form into 12 balls and roll in toasted coconut. Refrigerate.

35 calories each
MAKES 12

COFFEE SPONGE

1 envelope unflavored
    gelatine
2 cups skim milk
1 Tb. instant coffee powder
⅛ tsp. salt
1 tsp. liquid sweetener OR

1 packet (1 gram) of con-
    centrated powdered
    sugar substitute
1 tsp. vanilla
2 eggs whites

Soften gelatine in milk in saucepan. Add coffee and heat, stirring, until gelatine and coffee are dissolved. Add salt and sweetener. Chill until slightly thickened. Add vanilla and fold in beaten egg whites. Chill until firm. Add 1 tablespoon of Grand Marnier with vanilla, if you wish.

40 calories per serving
SERVES 6

HOLIDAY APRICOT CRÈME

4 cans (1 lb. each) dietetic
    canned apricots, drained
2 Tbs. apricot brandy
2 Tbs. liquid sweetener OR
6 (1 gram) packets concen-
    trated powdered sugar
    substitute OR
20 drops liquid concentrate

2 envelopes unflavored
    gelatine
¼ cup cold water
4 egg whites
1 tsp. vanilla
¼ cup nonfat dry milk
¼ cup ice water
5 ladyfingers, split

Purée 3 cans of apricots in an electric blender or through a sieve; add brandy and sweetener. Soften gelatine in cold water. Add to apricot purée, blending well. Beat egg whites and vanilla until stiff peaks form; beat gently into gelatine. Combine dry milk and ice water. Beat on high speed of mixer until mixture holds shape. Fold into apricot mixture. Line side of compote or serving dish with ladyfingers; spoon in apricot mixture and chill until set. Garnish with remaining can of apricot halves.

104 calories per serving
SERVES 10

LEMON CHIFFON PIE

10 graham crackers, finely
   crushed
2 Tbs. butter, melted

1 tsp. concentrated powdered
   sugar substitute or 10
   drops of liquid concentrate

Combine all ingredients, mix well, and press into 8- or
9-inch pie pan. Chill.

Lemon Filling

4 egg yolks, beaten
1½ Tbs. concentrated
   powdered sugar
   substitute OR
   15 drops liquid con-
   centrate
½ tsp. salt

3 Tbs. lemon juice
1 tsp. grated lemon rind
1 envelope unflavored
   gelatine
¼ cup cold water
4 egg whites

Combine egg yolks, sugar substitute, salt, lemon juice,
and rind in top of double boiler. Cook, beating with rotary
beater until thick, about 5 minutes. Soften gelatine in the
cold water and dissolve in hot mixture. Cool. Beat egg
whites until stiff but not dry and fold into lemon mixture.
Pour into pie shell and chill until firm.

101 calories per ⅛ of pie
SERVES 8

ORANGE BREAD PUDDING

4 slices diet bread, cubed
3 eggs, beaten
8 tsps. liquid sweetener OR
8 (1 gram) packets concentrated powdered sugar
   substitute OR
1 tsp. liquid concentrate
   drops

1½ cups orange juice
¼ tsp. salt
¼ cup shredded coconut
1 tsp. vanilla
2 Tbs. raisins

Preheat oven to 350° F.

Lightly butter a 1-quart casserole. Place bread cubes in
casserole. Combine remaining ingredients; pour over bread

and mix lightly. Place in pan of hot water and bake for from 45 to 60 minutes or until knife inserted comes out clean.

119 calories per serving
SERVES 6

BAKED APRICOT WHIP

¾ cup cooked dried apricots, sieved or puréed in blender
4 egg whites, beaten stiff

Dash of salt
1 tsp. vanilla
3 Tbs. honey

Preheat oven to 350° F.

Fold apricot purée into egg whites. Add salt, honey, and vanilla and mix lightly. Pile into 1-quart casserole and bake for about 20 minutes.

92 calories per serving
SERVES 6

BAKED CUSTARD

3 eggs
10 packets (1 gram each) of concentrated powdered sugar substitute OR
2 tsps. liquid sweetener OR

¾ tsp. liquid concentrate drops sweetener
⅛ tsp. salt
1 tsp. vanilla
2 cups scalded skim milk

Preheat oven to 300° F.

Combine eggs, sugar substitute, salt, and vanilla; mix well. Gradually add scalded milk, blending well. Pour into lightly greased pudding dish or four individual custard cups. Place custard dish or cups in a pan of hot water and bake 1 hour. Custard is finished when silver knife inserted in center comes out clean. Sprinkle with grated nutmeg.

81 calories
SERVES 4

CHOCO-MOCHA CREAM DREAM

¼ cup evaporated milk, whipped

1 envelope unflavored gelatine

¼ cup cold water

8 packets (1 gram each) concentrated powdered sugar substitute OR

2½ tsps. liquid sweetener OR

1 tsp. liquid concentrate drops

1 square or 1 envelope of unsweetened chocolate

1 cup skim milk

½ cup cold strong coffee

2 eggs, separated

1 tsp. vanilla

Chill evaporated milk in freezer until ice crystals form around edge. While milk is chilling, soften gelatine in cold water. Combine sugar substitute, chocolate, milk, and coffee in saucepan. Bring mixture to a boil. Remove from heat immediately. Beat egg yolks lightly. Add and return mixture to saucepan, cook over low heat, stirring constantly, for 1 minute. Remove from heat and add softened gelatine and vanilla. Mix thoroughly; cool. When cold and beginning to set, fold in stiffly beaten egg whites and the chilled evaporated milk whipped stiff with rotary beater. Spoon either into individual dishes or one large pudding dish. Chill.

56 calories per serving
SERVES 6

FROZEN TUTTI FRUTTI

½ cup evaporated milk

1 cup mashed bananas

1 can (9-oz.) crushed pineapple, well drained

½ cup chopped pecans

¼ cup powdered sugar substitute OR

10 packets (1 gram each) of concentrated powdered sugar substitute OR

1 tsp. liquid concentrate drops

¼ cup maraschino cherries, cut up and drained

1 Tb. lemon juice

Chill evaporated milk in ice tray until almost frozen at edges or put in freezing compartment for ½ hour in can. Mix bananas, pineapple, pecans, and sugar substitute, cherries, and lemon juice in bowl. Put ice-cold milk in electric mixer and beat at high speed until stiff. Fold in fruit mixture. Put in 1-quart container and freeze until firm.

90 calories

SERVES 6

LEMON MERINGUE DESSERT

3 Tbs. cornstarch	2 tsps. liquid sweetener
1 Tb. grated lemon peel	3 egg yolks
1½ cups water	1 Tb. butter
6 Tbs. lemon juice	
1½ tsps. concentrated powdered sugar substitute OR	

Place cornstarch and lemon peel in a saucepan. Blend water, lemon juice, sugar substitute, and egg yolks together. Gradually add to cornstarch and peel to make smooth paste. Cook over low heat, stirring constantly until thick. Stir in butter. Spoon into small (8-inch) casserole.

Meringue

3 egg whites	½ tsp. concentrated powdered
½ tsp. cream of tartar	sugar substitute
1 Tb. sugar*	

Preheat oven to 400° F.

Beat egg whites until foamy. Add cream of tartar and beat until stiff. Gradually add sugar and/or sugar substitute. Beat until glossy and stiff. Spoon over lemon mixture and bake for 5 minutes.

89 calories per serving

SERVES 6

* If you wish to eliminate sugar altogether use 1½ teaspoons of substitute and no sugar.

RUBY ICE

2 packages (10-oz.) of frozen   8 drops of liquid concentrate
   raspberries, thawed
2 egg whites
2 packets (1 gram each) of
   concentrated powdered
   sugar substitute OR

Press raspberries through a sieve and throw away the seeds. Beat egg whites until soft peaks form. Beating constantly, slowly add sugar substitute. Beat until peaks stiffen. Fold raspberry purée into this meringue. Freeze in medium-size bowl in freezer or freezing compartment. Stir occasionally until consistency of soft sherbet. Serve in chilled dishes.

80 calories
SERVES 6

SPONGE CUPCAKES

½ cup sifted cake flour   4 packets (1 gram each)
½ tsp. baking powder   concentrated powdered
⅛ tsp. salt   sugar substitute
1 egg, separated   ½ tsp. vanilla extract
¼ cup cold water   ¼ tsp. lemon extract
⅓ cup sifted granulated sugar

Preheat oven to 350° F.
Line 12, 2½" cupcake cups with packaged paper liners. Sift together flour, baking powder, and salt. Beat egg yolk with water until fluffy and tripled in volume. Add sugar gradually while still beating. Continue to beat until light-colored and thick enough to mound slightly—about 10 minutes. Stir in sugar substitute and extracts. Then add flour mixture, all at once, folding it in with a rubber spatula. Beat egg white until it stands in moist peaks when beater is

raised; then fold into yolk mixture with a rubber spatula until completely blended. Pour into cupcake cups. Divide batter evenly. Bake 15 minutes or until done.

43 calories per cupcake

YIELD: 12

MOUSSE AU CHOCOLAT

8 oz. semisweet chocolate	5 eggs, separated
½ oz. unsweetened chocolate	1 tsp. vanilla
¼ cup water	

Melt semisweet chocolate and unsweetened chocolate in water. Stir until blended. Remove from heat. Add egg yolks well beaten and vanilla. Beat egg whites until stiff and fold in chocolate mixture gently. Pour mousse into individual glasses and chill for 6 to 8 hours.

100 calories

SERVES 6

POACHED ORANGES

6 naval oranges	¾ cup water
3 Tbs. slivered orange rind	2 Tbs. Grand Marnier or
1½ cups sugar	Cointreau

Peel the rind and white membranes from oranges. Slice enough orange rind to make the three tablespoons of slivers and combine them with sugar and water. Cook syrup for about 8 minutes. Put whole oranges in syrup and cook them over low heat, basting constantly for about 5 minutes, or until warm but still firm. Remove them from heat and add liqueur. Chill and baste from time to time. Serve very cold.

175 calories

SERVES 6

APPLE PIE

½ cup cottage cheese   ⅛ tsp. salt
⅓ cup sifted flour   2 Tbs. shortening

Use a cheesecloth to squeeze cottage cheese dry. Sieve. Cut shortening into dry ingredients for regular crust. Add cottage cheese, mixing lightly with fork until ball of dough is formed. Turn out on very lightly floured cloth and roll to fit 9-inch pie shell. Makes 1 crust. Double ingredients for 2 crusts.

Filling

6 cups apples peeled and   1 tsp. lemon juice
  sliced   1 tsp. cinnamon
9 packets (1 gram each) con- 1 tsp. butter
  centrated powdered sugar
  substitute

Preheat oven to 350° F.

Arrange apples in 9-inch pie shell. Sprinkle sugar substitute, juice, cinnamon and dot butter over apples. Put the other crust arranged over the apples. Bake very slowly for 1 hour.

119 calories per ⅙ of pie
Serves 6

GRAPE DELIGHT

2 cups low-calorie grape drink 1 cup whole, unsweetened
1 envelope low-calorie straw-   strawberries
  berry gelatine

Pour 1 cup boiling grape drink over gelatine and stir until dissolved. Add remaining grape drink and chill mixture until it is the consistency of unbeaten egg whites. Fold in strawberries and pour into 4 serving dishes; chill until firm.

Topping

¼ cup low-calorie whipped   ¼ cup water
  topping mix   ¼ tsp. vanilla

Combine ingredients as directed on topping-mix package. Garnish each dessert with topping.

57 calories per serving, or 36 calories without topping

SERVES 4

PUMPKIN-PECAN PUDDING

1½ cups canned pumpkin
1 Tb. liquid sweetener
1 tsp. cinnamon
½ tsp. nutmeg

¼ cup chopped pecans
4 egg whites
⅛ tsp. salt

Preheat oven to 300° F.

Combine pumpkin, liquid sweetener, cinnamon, nutmeg, and pecans. Beat egg whites until foamy; add salt and beat until stiff peaks form. Blend ¼ of the beaten egg whites into the pumpkin mixture; then carefully fold in the remaining egg whites. Spoon into a 1-quart casserole. Set in a pan of hot water and bake 1 hour and 15 minutes, or until done.

64 calories per serving

SERVES 6

OLD-FASHIONED FRUIT PUDDING

1 can (1-lb.) diet apricot halves
1 can (1-lb.) diet Kadota figs
1 can (1-lb.) diet Royal Anne cherries

1 can (8-oz.) diet Bartlett pears
1½ Tbs. liquid sweetener
4 Tbs. quick-cooking tapioca

Drain fruits, saving liquid. Place fruits in a dessert bowl. Measure 2 cups of the combined liquids; pour into a saucepan. Add sweetener and tapioca; let stand 5 minutes. Cook, stirring constantly until thick and clear. Pour sauce over fruit. Chill. If desired, serve with Custard Sauce.

104 calories per serving

SERVES 8

APRICOT RICE PUDDING

1 can (1-lb.) peeled apricots,
    dietetic
⅔ cup packaged precooked
    rice
¼ tsp. salt

2 Tbs. lemon juice
1 tsp. cinnamon
½ tsp. nutmeg
1 Tb. butter or margarine

Quarter apricots. In a 1-quart casserole combine rice, salt, lemon juice, apricot pieces, and syrup from apricots. Sprinkle with cinnamon and nutmeg; dot with butter. Bake 20 to 25 minutes or until rice is tender. Serve warm.

95 calories per serving
SERVES 4

CUSTARD SAUCE

2 eggs, well beaten
1½ tsps. liquid sweetener
    Pinch of salt

¾ cup skim milk, scalded
½ tsp. vanilla (or other fla-
    voring)

In top of double boiler, combine beaten eggs, sweetener, and salt. Stir in scalded milk gradually. Cook over hot (not boiling) water, stirring frequently only until mixture begins to thicken slightly (about 15 minutes).

Immediately remove from heat; pour into heat-proof bowl, and stir in flavoring. Place immediately in refrigerator to chill rapidly. Custard thickens more as it chills.

27 calories per serving
SERVES 8

PEACH BLENDELICIOUS

1 can (1-lb.) sliced peaches
    (2 cups)
1 Tb. lemon juice
1 envelope unflavored
    gelatine

½ cup cold water
2 egg whites

Put fruit and lemon juice in blender. Cover and blend

for 4 seconds. Soften gelatine in cold water; then heat until gelatine is dissolved. Add to fruit in container. Cover and blend for 2 seconds. Let stand for 5 minutes. Add 1 unbeaten egg white; cover and blend for 10 seconds. Add second egg white; cover and blend until frothy. Pour into individual dishes and chill.

80 calories per serving
40 calories if diet fruit used
Serves 6

CHERRY-BERRY CRUMBLE

1 can (1-lb.) water-pack red sour cherries	¼ cup quick-cooking tapioca
1 package (10-oz.) frozen unsweetened blueberries	1½ Tbs. liquid sweetener
	2 Tbs. lemon juice

Preheat oven to 350° F.

Drain cherries; measure liquid and add enough water to make 1½ cups. Combine cherries and blueberries in a shallow 1-quart casserole. In a saucepan, combine tapioca, liquid sweetener, lemon juice, and cherry liquid. Cook over medium heat, stirring constantly, until tapioca is cooked and mixture is thickened. Pour over fruit in casserole. Bake 10 minutes. Remove from oven.

Topping

8 small graham crackers, crushed	1 Tb. melted butter
1 tsp. grated lemon rind	¾ tsp. liquid sweetener

Combine all ingredients for topping; mix well and sprinkle over partially cooked fruit; return to oven and bake 10 minutes longer.

124 calories per serving (with sugar 251 calories)
Serves 6

BERRY BLEND-A-FREEZE

2 packages frozen red rasp-   ½ cup yogurt
   berries   ½ tsp. vanilla
1 Tb. Grand Marnier

Put berries, Grand Marnier, and juice from berries in blender. Cover and blend 30 seconds, until smooth. Pour into ice-cube tray. Spoon yogurt mixed with vanilla over top of berries. Freeze.

100 calories per serving
50 if diet fruit used
SERVES 5

BANANA CRÈME

2 envelopes unflavored   1 Tb. lemon juice
   gelatine   ¼ cup sherry
1¼ cups water   4 medium bananas, mashed
1 cup orange juice   ⅓ cup nonfat dry milk
2 Tbs. liquid sweetener ⅓ cup ice water

Soften gelatine in ¼ cup of the water. Bring remaining 1 cup water to a boil; add to gelatine, stirring to dissolve. Add orange juice, sweetener, lemon juice, and sherry. Blend in bananas. Chill until mixture begins to set. Combine dry milk and ice water; beat on high speed of mixer until peaks form. Fold into gelatine. Spoon into a 6-cup mold. Chill and set.

95 calories per serving
SERVES 8

COCONUT BANANA BAKE
Best Diet Dessert

3 large bananas   ⅓ cup shredded coconut
1½ Tbs. melted butter   ½ tsp. sherry
2 Tbs. lemon or lime juice

Preheat oven to 375° F.

Select green-tipped or yellow bananas. Peel. Split length-wise and then cut in half. Lay in greased 10″ × 6″ × 2″ pan. Melt butter and brush bananas with mixture of butter and lemon or lime juice. Sprinkle top with coconut and sherry. Bake 15 to 20 minutes or until soft when pierced with fork. Serve warm, plain or with Dieter's Orange Sauce.

104 calories

SERVES 6

DIETER'S ORANGE SAUCE

⅓ cup sugar
1 Tb. cornstarch
  Pinch of salt
⅛ tsp. cinnamon
⅔ cup boiling water

2 Tbs. butter
1 tsp. grated orange rind
¼ cup orange juice
1 Tb. lemon juice

Combine first four ingredients in saucepan and add boiling water. Bring to boil stirring constantly until mixture thickens. Stir in butter, rind, juices. Serve warm.

58 calories

SODA BAKED APPLES

4 tart apples
½ tsp. cinnamon
¼ cup raisins

1 bottle (7-oz.) diet grape, orange, black cherry, cola

Preheat oven to 375° F.

Pick good-sized apples. Core about half of each apple and peel one third of the top. Place in deep-sided pan large enough to fit the apples. Fill cavity made by coring with raisins. Sprinkle with cinnamon. Pour diet soda over apples and bake, covered, for ½ hour, basting periodically until baking period is over. Remove cover and continue baking and basting for another ½ hour, or until apples are soft when tested with a fork.

100 calories per serving

SERVES 4

EMPEROR'S DESSERT

⅔ cup sugar
⅔ cup water
4 tsps. fresh lemon juice
6 unpeeled fresh pears

2 cups Emperor grapes,
   seeded
½ cup white wine or gingerale
   (diet)

Combine sugar, water, and lemon juice in saucepan. Cut pears in quarters lengthwise and add. Cover and bring to boiling point. Simmer 3 to 5 minutes. Remove pears from heat and cool. Combine pears and syrup with grapes and white wine. Chill. Serve in fruit dishes.

90 calories per serving
SERVES 6

SUNFLOWER SALAD DESSERT

1 can (1 lb. 1 oz.) low-calorie
   fruit cocktail
3 envelopes lemon-flavored
   diet gelatine

2 cups hot water
1 medium orange

Drain fruit cocktail and reserve syrup. Dissolve gelatine in hot water. Add enough cold water to reserved syrup to make 1 cup; add to gelatine. Cut orange in half slices. Arrange around the sides of 9″ round pan with curved edge facing outside. Fill center with drained fruit cocktail. Carefully pour 1 cup gelatine over fruit. Chill until almost set. Pour remaining gelatine over. Chill until firm.

30 calories per serving
SERVES 8

BIBLIOGRAPHY

The Delectable Past, ESTHER ARESTY (Simon and Schuster)
Collation of Cakes, CLAUDIA Q. MURPHY
Larousse's Gastronomique (Crown)
Gourmet Magazine
Dessert to the True American, Microfilm, Library of Congress
Desserts, Charles Francatelli's Rare Book Collection, Library of Congress
Cooks, Gluttons and Gourmets, BETTY WASON (Doubleday)
Encyclopaedia of European Cooking, MUSIA SOPER (Radio City)
The Art of Fine Baking, PAULA PECK (Simon and Schuster)
Encyclopaedia Britannica
World Book

INDEX